Deadlines and
DATELINES

Tales and travails of a *Times* foreign correspondent

CHRISTOPHER THOMAS

Quadrant Books

First published in 2021 by Quadrant Books
A member of the Memoirs Group
Suite 2, Top Floor, 7 Dyer Street, Cirencester, Gloucestershire, GL7 2PF

Copyright ©Christopher Thomas 2021
Christopher Thomas has asserted his right under the Copyright Designs and Patents
Act 1988 to be identified as the author of this work.

The moral right of the author has been asserted by them in
accordance with the Copyright, Designs and Patents Act, 1988
All rights reserved.

No part of this publication may be reproduced, stored in a retrieval
system, or transmitted in any form or by any means, without the prior
permission in writing of the publisher, nor be otherwise circulated in
any form of binding or cover other than that in which it is published
and without a similar condition including this condition being imposed
on the subsequent purchaser

Reasonable efforts have been made to find the copyright holders of
any third party copyright material. An appropriate acknowledgement can
be inserted by the publisher in any subsequent printing or edition

A catalogue record for this book is available from the British Library

Deadlines and datelines
Paperback ISBN 978-1-86151-049-5

Typeset by Ray Lipscombe Design, Cirencester
Printed and bound in Great Britain

To Valerie, my wife.

To Melanie, Maria and Matthew, my children.

My thanks to Penny Riley, whose editing and encouragement were crucial.

INTRODUCTION

This chronicle is mostly about my life as a journalist, the only job I ever did after graduating from tea-boy on a local paper. I worked for *The Times* for 28 years, most of them as a foreign correspondent, often disappearing for weeks and occasionally months. Big newspapers had money to burn back then, before succumbing to the Internet.

In the telling of some of my stories – a small selection, or there would be no end to it – I reminded myself that time makes liars of us all, so I have made every effort to be accurate. My newspaper cuttings were a vital diary, reminding me of names, dates and places in 41 countries I reported from. Memories flooded back whenever I read them.

Knowing or sensing that a story is out there, getting to it, nailing it down and then filing it to London in sometimes challenging conditions, and to know it's heading for a good show in the next day's paper – that's a thrill you can't buy. I wouldn't have chosen another life.

Every day during our 20 years abroad Valerie scoured *The Times* for my articles and pasted them into scrapbooks. She was fanatical about this. If a paper containing a story of mine went missing she would order another copy from London and pester them until she got it. She knew what she was doing: she was planning. She owns this book.

CHAPTER ONE

There is a long mirror in the tiny bedroom I share with my brother. I have posed myself meticulously before it. Through an open window behind me I hear sheets flapping on a washing line stretched the length of our small suburban garden in an unremarkable place called Corringham, in Essex. It's been raining for days; they'll never dry. To north, east and west of our bungalow, in thousands and thousands of similar streets, houses drip gloomily in the rain. To the south, the River Thames passes by the cement factory, the docks and the oil refinery.

The bedroom is quiet. Nobody is home. I have prepared myself carefully, camera in one hand, notebook in the other, pencil behind my ear, coat collar turned high, hair tousled. The war is getting closer. Time to run. It is fiercely hot here in this bombed-out desert town, and a stiff breeze throws sand into my face. From all sides there are explosions. Rival

1

militia are battling street by street. There is tank-fire. Filthy black smoke blocks the sun. Bullets puff into the ground left and right of me. Bodies are strewn like garbage. Somebody is screaming, 'get down!' I don't know if it's a threat or a warning, but I ignore it because I must discover what is happening, for I am – cry it loudly – a foreign correspondent!

Back then, when not yet a teenager, I believed those evocative two words described somebody on a moral mission who didn't mind a bit of loneliness in bold and relentless pursuit of *the truth*. And here was I, flying through hellfire, being that very person. It turned out never to be quite like that – or *anything* like that – but it was a grand fantasy for an 11-year-old with early-onset acne, an appalling education that mostly stopped at that age, an accent that was low-grade cor-blimey (accents mattered a lot more back then), who had never been further than the Isle of Wight and was burdened with a headful of emotional problems gifted by a perfectly mad mother.

I stumbled through my early years hearing two voices, one loud and parental saying I was useless and would come to nothing, the other quietly in my head saying I wasn't and wouldn't. My dream of being a journalist was a secret friend, providing focus, purpose and safety during the turbulent years of youth. We were inseparable. There was hardly any likelihood of the dream coming true, but I didn't know that and held it fiercely tight, squeezing every sweet drop out of it until doors that had never existed swung open and all sorts of extraordinary coincidences conspired to make it real.

My ambitions were never enormous: I was never going

to own big or change anything big or get rich big. I just wanted to do something different with my life, and that felt big enough. Those words 'foreign correspondent' were my mantra. The mirror fantasies were crucial because they gave clarity. If you can't imagine it, you can't have it. Or, as a philosophical wag put it, if you don't have a target in life, you're bound to hit it. Perhaps old man Fate needs to see your dreams over and over, year after year, before granting them, or perhaps in my case he got bored with my insane persistence and said 'for pity's sake here you are, now go away'. Who knows how it all works? Nothing is but thinking makes it so. Maybe that's it. Henry Ford put it well: 'If you think you can, or if you think you can't, you're right.'

My first awareness of a desire – a need, a hunger, a rage – to be a journalist and thence a foreign correspondent began with an American TV series called *Man of the World*, depicting a freelance photo-journalist who travelled the world in a yacht. He had everything I sought. I was still a child, around 10, who shouldn't have been thinking of escapism, but it was the only way to handle the farce of family life my brother Michael and I had to get through. He spent his time out with friends and I spent mine floating in the clouds. I was never one for being around lots of people.

That guy on the TV, all charm and manly confidence as he sailed single-handed towards his next assignment, was his own master, coming and going as he chose, no boss, no routine, totally devoted to what he did. It was a silly programme with no concession to reality, but it fed my nascent hunger for adventure and freedom. I kept those

3

feelings to myself, however. Being a dreamer and romancer was not something to be lightly confessed in the no-nonsense world I occupied, so I lived a private life. I got a warning shot when I overheard a relative opining, 'Out with the fairies, that one. Always in his own head.'

I did once nervously tell a teacher when I was 12 that I wanted to be a reporter and a foreign correspondent, and he nearly passed out laughing. I don't think teaching was his true vocation. 'Christ, boy, remember who you are, a secondary modern school reject in a sink school called Hassenbrook in Stanford-le-Hope in Essex.' Those weren't his actual words, but that was the essence of what he said.

It's a wonder I got to speak to him at all, because there were 52 kids in my class. It wasn't education, it was crowd control until you served your time and stepped aside for the next wave of 11-plus failures (of which I was one). One of our teachers used to walk around the classroom brandishing a baseball bat which he would bang loudly across our desks, making kids cry. Weirdly, he called it his ham sandwich. He never used it on anybody to my knowledge, but it hovered about us like a threat. Nobody in authority cared. It was that kind of place.

The school now calls itself Hassenbrook Academy, and its official website declares: 'The beauty of Hassenbrook Academy is that we pride ourselves on being small enough to care yet big enough to make a huge impact on the lives of all of our students.' Gosh. I couldn't resist checking an up-to-date Ofsted report into this magical place, only to discover that it was still a crap school subject to 'special measures'. There was some stuff about the emergence of 'green shoots' and 'initial signs of improving standards.' Hang on, I was there two generations ago – green shoots? No oaks then? Let's be honest, it wasn't a school, it was a processing centre.

On my first day in this place, aged 11, the headmaster stood on the stage in front of 1,200 of us and, dull as a dirge, intoned, 'The fact that you have come to this school doesn't mean you are failures.' Oh no? Those few words hit like a slap and I am certain my recall is word perfect. I remember the big hall through which they echoed, the high windows, the long curtains on the stage where he stood in front of a microphone, the sound and smell of massed youth on their first restless day of internment in the final school of their lives. Of all the words he might have chosen on that day to reassure us, he chose the worst. We all heard the lie in them.

I knew for certain at that moment that I was destined for a life that frightened me, or, to put it another way, my father's life, which even he thought of as a demi-life. I know that's true because years later he told me he had just paid the last mortgage instalment on his two-bedroom bungalow after 25 years, and his eyes watered when I asked if he felt a sense of achievement. He muttered something inaudible and turned away. He wasn't much of a talker, my dad, but no words could have better articulated the waste he felt. Depression stalked the last years of his truncated life.

The headmaster summoned a black man from the corner of the stage and appealed to us to ask if any of our parents might provide him with lodgings because he was a newly recruited teacher with nowhere to live. It was a shamefully crass thing to do in front of all us kids, knowing as he surely must that racism was a local sport.

The poor man looked out at the sea of young foreigners and I could feel his bewilderment and humiliation as he was exhibited like a rare species, which he was, back then. I could have sobbed for him when sniggering burst into laughter while the hapless headmaster hollered for silence. Derision and mockery swamped the man as he returned to the corner of the stage, and I bet he wept that night. No matter if he didn't because I did it for him.

His spoken English was terrible – I think he was Caribbean – but he filled a teaching slot that might have been hard to fill in a school like Hassenbrook. What he never did, it can be assumed, is teach very much to anybody. Nobody ever taught us boys anything much beyond woodwork or metal-work (I was spectacularly useless at both) or something to do with mechanics (ditto) – and if you were a girl your career options didn't extend much beyond shop-keeping. Good old Hassenbrook. It remains true to itself to this day. But, in fairness, it must be immeasurably better than it was. It could not be otherwise.

A certain Mr Spencer, headmaster of a desperately over-subscribed junior school in Stanford-le-Hope which I had lately left – an entirely wooden building, built as a temporary 'overflow' structure to cope with the post-war 'surge' of us, its six classrooms packed to bursting – told my parents flatly, to their faces, that I would not pass the

11-plus examination, the gateway to grammar school and from there to university. His deputy was none other than Mrs Spencer, and together they were well acquainted with the social provenance of their young charges. My destiny was Hassenbrook, where the bluest of blue-collar kids went. If I had been Einstein himself, I would have failed.

Young as I was, I knew all about the post-war surge of children who were overwhelming the school system, and we were described in ways that gave some of us feelings of being surplus to requirement. They called us 'the bulge,' like an unpleasant swelling, or 'the overflow,' or even, hideously, a 'glut.' What rotten labels to hang onto a generation of kids. This, and the stigma of failure, drifted among all the kids in Hassenbrook like a bad smell, creating attitudes that ranged from sycophancy (others know what's good for us) to aggression (fuck the world), and for some it set the stage for a life-long bitterness hard as cement.

Those who passed the 11-plus received a letter bearing official words of congratulations. Teachers slapped the victorious children's backs in the playground, while Mr and Mrs Spencer presented themselves to receive several delighted parents. I see the scene clearly: parents hugging their triumphant children and pumping the hands of the beaming Spencers. We losers, by far the majority, stood aside, spectators of our own failure, eyes down, ashamed. We hoped our letters would come in the second post (there was one back then) but of course they didn't. We were rejected summarily and silently, not worth a stamp or an envelope or a kindly lie about how well we had done.

'Have you had your letter?' some boy asked me.

'No, not yet.'

'Too bad. I'm off to Palmers.' Back home later that day, when I informed my mother of the terrible news, she beat me with her favourite instrument, a hard slipper. I don't remember what my father said or did, so perhaps he said and did nothing. He was always a non-presence, a shadow moving in and out of the house on his constant shift-work rota, and seemed never to be around when I was. Not a soul in my acquaintance passed the 11-plus and went to Palmers, the local grammar school. The class divide was sharp as a blade.

Palmers: the word dripped with mystique. The school – there were actually two of them, one each for boys and girls – occupied buildings of classical beauty that were knocked down years later because that's the sort of thing the crapulous morons of Thurrock Council did. They loved no building not made of cement.

When I was 17 and a year into my first job I met Mrs Spencer, by then retired. She was cycling through my home-town of Corringham (she lived in the best part in a bungalow opposite the recreation ground) and amazingly recognised me in the street. She stopped to ask where I was working. When I told her I was a trainee reporter on the local paper she looked startled, because that was Palmers-boy territory. 'Oh,' she said, muttered some words of congratulations, and wobbled off down the road. That felt good.

My dad worked at the nearby Shell oil refinery alongside the

River Thames at a place called Coryton, and read the *Daily Mirror* and cowboy novels when there was nothing going on. All his working life he did a rota of three shifts, each lasting about a week. That meant he never had a proper night's sleep and only occasionally had a proper meal, which probably precipitated his death at 65 from a heart attack. He was called a 'jettyman'. He connected pipelines to ships, through which crude oil was pumped into huge storage tanks, and he did that for 40 years.

When I was working on the local paper I was invited by the Public Relations Officer at the Shell oil refinery – a Mr Black – to go on a tour of the complex and the neighbouring oil storage unit, Thames Haven. He said a car would pick me up, and when it came it was a limousine with a be-suited driver who opened the back door and stood aside for me to get in. I sat up front. I was 17 for God's sake!

As Mr Black and I walked around the refinery I stopped dead at the sight of a man in blue overalls, who stared back at me incredulously. He didn't acknowledge me in any way except with his shock reaction: no greeting, no wave, no word, just his eyes burning into me as I stood there, all done up in suit and tie, being escorted around by a member of management. It was my dad. He turned and walked off to the wooden hut that he and his co-workers shared at the end of the jetty. I had inadvertently done something awful. I had invaded his private world, his refuge, his hiding place from life at home with an unstable wife, the one place where he was safe and popular among friends who quietly understood his plight. I had no right to see it.

I was taken to the executive dining room for lunch and sipped gently at a bowl of very thin, cold soup with a piece of lemon floating in it. I don't suppose I was the first person ever to spoon down the water from the finger bowl. I was also given a glass of wine, the very first alcohol I had ever tasted, and it hit me hard. I was quite tipsy when I clambered into the limousine for the return journey, and this time I took the back seat.

The next time I tasted alcohol was a carefully planned affair after I turned 18. Booze had never interested me, because every Christmas I had watched people make spectacles of themselves when they fell over sofas or started fighting or, on one occasion, by tipping a rum-and-blackcurrant cocktail over my parent's brand-new cream-coloured fitted carpet, then rubbing it in nice and deep with a handkerchief to ensure it would remain for ever. That stain followed me all the way through my childhood and early teens.

Having reached the legal age to go into a pub, I decided I had to give grog a go and randomly chose the location for this momentous coming-of-age, namely the Railway Hotel in Stanford-le-Hope. It was a miserable dive. I ordered half a pint of beer, which I carried to a table in the corner for this rather private moment. It tasted ghastly, but I eventually got the hang of the stuff and became a life-long beer drinker with little affection for wine and none for hard liquor.

Apart from the Bible my mother read only knitting patterns and *Woman* magazine and was a farmworker for many years before changing to factory work. My earliest school holidays were spent in the fields with her, and the freedom to explore the land made for happy days – the happiest period of my childhood. The smell of turned earth, along with heaps of mud-covered potatoes lying on the surface like jewels dragged from secret depths, remain a powerful memory. Smells, it seems to me, are scrupulously honest in evoking old feelings. Time distorts memories, but never does it tamper with the memory of a smell.

Farmer Young was an old-fashioned bachelor who still had working horses and I got to sit on them and even drive a horse and cart sometimes. Chemicals hadn't been introduced yet, at least not on his farm, and half a dozen women – including my mother – spent eight hours a day hoeing weeds from serried rows of crops, half crippled by backache by the time they went home. My mother was an accomplished thief: she nicked tons of vegetables over the years without ever getting caught. She would stack them into the basket on the front of her bicycle, cover them with something, and pedal off at a frantic rate like a night thief. I suspect Farmer Young was fully aware of the larceny.

She moved from there to a shoe factory in East Tilbury called Bata, working at a clattering sewing machine that sounded like a landing helicopter. I saw her there once, hunched over this huge machine among row upon row of them, and the noise was inhumane. The workers, all women, had an hour for lunch and a couple of 20-minute tea breaks in an eight-hour shift. If anybody needed an unscheduled toilet break they had to raise their hand for permission from the forelady. They looked like POWs doing forced labour.

My mother came home by bus every night, still wrapped

in her blue works apron, ranting about 'Elsie the Forelady', who sounded worse than Torquemada having a bad day. 'So I says to her I says... and she says to me... so I says to her... and she says to me...' It was all she ever seemed to talk to my dad about, except to lay out orders for DIY jobs she wanted done. I think it was why he chose to do shift work.

Elsie, this despicable woman obsessively monitoring individual productivity with pad and pen and lashing people with disagreeable comments – my mother's version of her – was part of the fabric of my childhood, but I never met her. Had I done so I would not have been the least surprised to find that she was a model of grace and charm. If it wasn't Elsie quivering on the end my mother's acerbic tongue it was 'her next door,' a woman called Doll who was always perfectly pleasant to my mind, but my mother took against her, as she did most people.

My mother left that job to become a canteen worker at the Shell refinery, where she honed her thieving skills to an art form. She was a good seamstress and stitched false linings into her coats like giant pockets, and every night went home weighed down with pilfered food. At 9am when she started work she was skinny. At 5pm when she heaved on her coat to go home, she was fat. Nobody at the security gate ever questioned her because she was stealing from the nobs, so they didn't care. Besides, they shared the booty.

I suppose I am of the last British generation who were scrubbed once a week in a tin bath in front of the fire (the water was always tepid and soapy because my brother, being three years older, got in first). The house was barely heated in the winter because of the cost, and only ever in the living room, so we all had to share this tiny space or freeze.

Coal became expensive, so they bought a paraffin heater that flared up lethally with any slight draught, and it's a wonder the house survived. The damn thing gave off stinking fumes that made our eyes water. I was regularly dispatched to the local garage with a gallon can to be half filled with paraffin, because that's all they could afford in one go. The mortgage was killing them and all the furniture was on hire purchase, which had to be repaid in cash to a man who called at the door once a week and wrote everything down in a big ledger.

Gran Ockendon, who lived not far away from our little two-bedroom bungalow, still had an outside privy, a scullery with a concrete scrubbing board, and no electricity. This was in the 1950s, not the 1900s or Orwell's 1930s. It was an old terraced house, unchanged from the day it was built. There were gaslights on the wall that left black smudges on the ceiling which peculiarly resembled the maps of countries, and the only heating was an open fire that was a bitch to ignite. How many times did Gran nearly burn the house down when holding newspapers against the wretched thing to get it to light? I see her now, dancing on the burning newspapers on the hearth, cursing like a stevedore six pints into Saturday night.

Every Sunday lunchtime I cycled down to her house to collect money to buy three pints of Guinness for her in Wood's off-licence nearby, an errand she rewarded with a handful of pennies and halfpennies removed from the pension she collected in cash from the Post Office every week. The money came in little brown envelopes with holes across the top so you could see the tantalising pound notes and ten bob notes inside. The coins in the bottom jingled like jewels. Gran's needs didn't extend much beyond Guinness and scotch (she had no time for food if it wasn't bread and cheese) so she didn't spend much, and when she died the family found a trove of unopened envelopes in the dark cupboard under the stairs. Lord knows which relative got to them, but they disappeared in a flash.

My mother never definitively worked out how Gran always had a bottle of whisky and ample bottles of Guinness on the go. The whisky was always tucked behind the cushion of her chair like a dirty secret and there would be hell to pay when my teetotal mother tried to confiscate it, because Gran had a stern temper, a strong arm and a fierce will, and they had screaming fights over it. The secret Samaritan was my Uncle Clarry, who never let her run dry. Gran always reimbursed him, plus a bit. He lived in poverty in his nearby council house and every winter moved into his kitchen with his mattress and TV and lit the gas cooker for warmth. He was a big-hearted tragic man with a funny accent, because earlier in life he had tried to teach himself to talk posh and made a hash of it.

Gran always called me 'boy' because she had trouble remembering my name. When she did remember it she pronounced it *Crisserfer*. She had been a farmworker since leaving school, until late in life she took a job as a cleaner in a shrimp-processing factory not far from home because hauling sacks of potatoes was getting a bit much. They forced her to retire when she was well into her seventies, and when they sent her a bouquet of flowers as a goodbye present she told the delivery boy to stick them up his backside and slammed the door in his face. What she wanted was her job back. She was very upset.

I never really knew many of my relatives, even though they lived nearby. Mostly we only met at family Christmas piss-ups. The liveliest of the bunch was Aunt Lil, who could sink more gin and tonics than it was possible to count and still talk sense. She used to call me a 'poor little cock'. I loved that. Her slot for the family round of Christmas debauchery was Boxing Day when everybody would get slaughtered on whisky and gin and oceans of beer, and in the early hours of the morning we'd wind our way out of her council house doing the hokey-cokey all the way down Laburnum Drive yelling Happy Christmas at the neighbours' curtained windows.

These bacchanals sometimes ended with a punch-up: I clearly remember one of my relatives punching another in the mouth for kissing his wife, and sending him crashing against a glass kitchen door that split into pieces. Before everybody got completely legless, however, Aunt Lil would make all the grown-ups play 'Oranges and Lemons The Bells of St Clements' with us kids and call us poor little cocks as we fell asleep on the sofas to the raucous sound of 20 inebriates.

When I introduced her to my 11-year-old son Matthew

years later she called him a poor little cock and offered him a cigarette. 'Do you good,' she said. She reached into a cupboard and gave me a glass and a miniature bottle of scotch and I saw dozens of miniatures in there, scotch and gin and brandy and vodka, the works. Where were they nicked from, I wondered? Aunt Lil went everywhere on her bicycle with a basket on the front, a chirpy little woman with a ready laugh, until her mind went and she had to go into care.

My dad wasn't above a bit of nicking. He regularly stole small quantities of petrol from work and poured it into a rainwater butt in the garage, and sometimes it was full to the brim. When we went on holiday, usually to a rented caravan or a low-end boarding house in Devon, he loaded the boot with cans of petrol while my brother and I squeezed among the suitcases on the back seat. We were a bomb on wheels. It took a day and a night to drive to Devon back then, and we would all spend one night in a lab-by in the car because there was no money for hotels.

Uncle Alf, who also worked at the Shell refinery, raced greyhounds, which he bred. His daughter Tricia was my inseparable best friend throughout our infancy, and still is my friend. Uncle Clive was what they called 'slow' and pushed around a tea trolley in a factory, where he was also responsible for changing light bulbs, which was the outer limit of his talents. He was weird and would get horribly drunk and maudlin. Never married, never left home, died in his 40s. He should have died a lot earlier, because he was always driving while blind drunk. He demolished a flower shop in Stanford-le-Hope when he missed a bend and drove straight into it on his way home from the Rising Sun pub, and when the police turned up they found him asleep among the tulips, totally uninjured amid tons of rubble.

But it was Gran Ockendon who I knew best of the adult relatives, and she was my friend. When she was a teenager she had a child out of wedlock called Percy, who was buried a few years later in the churchyard at St. Margaret's Church, in the Essex village of Fobbing. She was thrown out of home in disgrace in one of those 'do not darken my doorstep again' family dramas. There was a lot of speculation about the father, but she never told. The family lodger raped her, so the gossip suggested, which may have been a ruse to absolve her of immorality. She was one of ten or more children in her family, several of whom died in – or from – poverty. Gran's last words, a few hours before she died, were: 'Hang on Percy, I'm coming.' He had been dead 60 years. Percy's grave was lost until my big-hearted second cousin, Yvonne, hunted it down and put the old Celtic cross back together.

At work Gran drove the horses, hoed weeds, picked potatoes or peas and did anything else Farmer Young told her to do, enduring all weathers in a career of something like 45 years tending his land. Mr Young died when a shire horse kicked him in the head. Gran never had a day's illness until a few weeks before she died, defying 20 cigarettes a day (a particularly toxic brand called Weights) and copious amounts of scotch, which had perforce entirely replaced Guinness due to a weakening bladder.

Despite her reputation for being an unwed mother, albeit

now childless, she found a husband in her 20s known as Buffa, and I have no idea where that nickname came from. He gave new meaning to the word 'taciturn': he could suck on roll-ups and watch the smoke drifting away for hour upon silent hour, sitting on a hard-back upright chair in his little living room, the light of the coal fire dancing in his magnificent head of silver hair. He kept dog-ends in the lining of his flat-cap until there were enough to roll another fag. I have a picture of him, and he was film star handsome.

Gran's birthday was on Christmas Eve – hence her name, Christine – and every year she occupied the Christmas Eve slot for the family party-round. I drove home with my dad after one of those binges and if I hadn't lunged at the steering wheel, child though I was, we would have gone into a lamppost because we were driving on the pavement. The amazing thing is that when we got home I heard Father Christmas passing overhead in his sleigh, bells and all. It was real as Christmas. My parents' slot for the season's partying was Christmas night, and my mother ran herself ragged all day making sandwiches and sausage rolls while my dad assembled tottering crates of booze from the floor half way to the ceiling – enough to ensure a katzenjammer for all.

I had the temerity to be born on Christmas Day, hence my name. This was very kind of Old Man Fate, because my parents were thinking of calling me John, unaware of what a John Thomas is. I slithered into the world in a rented two-bedroom terraced house in Digby Road, Corringham, which she and my dad eventually bought for around £2,000. According to my mother the midwife turned up drunk, Gran was sleeping off her lunchtime indulgences in the next room, and my dad was at the pub celebrating my imminent birth, which was so imminent he missed it.

My mother used to wheel a toothless and decayed old poodle called Mitzi around Corringham in a push-chair, tucked up in pink blankets with a bow in its top-knot, stinking like a corpse, and people would be taken aback when they went to coo at a baby and found an ancient dog instead.

'Seventeen years old,' they would be told. The dog was buried in the back garden in an oak coffin with brass handles, silk lining and a silver crucifix around its neck. The undertakers had made it to order, and I bet they had a good laugh when she gave them the dog's photograph so they could get the measurements right. Neighbours were invited to come and see the corpse and offer prayers, but I don't think any did. The vicar from St Mary's declined my mother's request to conduct a service for Mitzi in church, although he did indulge her by visiting the house and giving the dog some sort of blessing. By then she was rock hard in her little casket, because my mother didn't want to part with her. I bet the priest questioned his vocation after that. My mother, Bible in one hand, crucifix in the other, wailed and prayed up a storm as my dad lowered the coffin into the grave she had made him dig in the garden, and her stirring performance had him sobbing with her. One day when somebody discovers the dog's bones there's going to be a massive police operation with forensic tents and TV coverage until experts rule out child murder.

One very cold night my mother gave me a particularly thorough thrashing with her slipper on my face and bare legs (my dad was at work; these frequent beatings never usually happened when he was home) for reasons lost to me, and threw me out of the house in a great drama in which she lamented, at piercing volume, the tragedy of her life in general and of my being a boy in particular, because she already had one of those and wanted a girl. Amazing how neighbours can be deaf. How she could yell.

She stuffed my pyjamas into my raincoat – I recall the feeling of her tightening the belt around me so they wouldn't fall out – and told me to go to the police station, which was in the next street, and tell them to put me away because I wasn't wanted. I suppose I was seven. Nobody answered when I knocked on the police station door, so I stood for a long time wondering what to do. I was getting very cold. Then my mother turned up. 'Go on,' she said, 'knock.' I told her I had. 'Then stay there till someone comes.' She went away, knowing that nobody would come because it was a part-time nick.

After a long time I was so cold I decided to walk to Gran's house about a mile away. Half way there my mother came roaring after me and slapped me around the head for leaving the police station. This happened on what used to be called Dane's Corner, where there was a grocery shop (owned by Mr Dane) that is now a cafe, opposite the little Church of England chapel that's now somebody's house.

I could identify the spot to the nearest yard. I was never more disappointed by anything in my young life than to be stopped by her on that day, because if I had reached Gran's house I might have been taken in. I was fully aware by then that my mother was crazy.

She tried hard to turn me into the girl I was meant to be. I was kept in a pram until I was so old I can just about remember being in it (not a pushchair but the real thing, with big sprung wheels and a large hood) and being told to stay in there while she wheeled me up and down the streets. I was swaddled in blankets, because underneath them I was in girl's clothes and she didn't want anybody to know. I don't remember those details, but relatives have told me about it.

When I went to school she dressed me in bright yellow jumpers and bright red short trousers, a crisp white shirt, a tie, and coloured socks with white bumpers (as trainers were called). I was brighter than a firework. Every Sunday on bath-night she put curlers in my hair and poured a thick green liquid on my head called Amami Wave Set and Conditioner. I can see the bottle now and smell that oily foul fluid. The boys at school gave me a hard time and I used to roll around in the dirt to man-up my clothes and tug at my knotted hair to straighten it. This continued, to my best recollection, until I was around eight or nine. My dad never intervened. Funny that.

It's the oddest thing: you come out of the other side of these experiences and start moving through life as a young man and what you desperately want is parental approval despite everything that has gone on, for them to say you're

21

doing well, proud of you lad, good on you. Is it a form of Stockholm Syndrome?

In my mid-teens I held conversations in which I imagined myself to be two people, like a chess-player playing himself. I would set us up to disagree with each other, forcing me to put words to feelings and to answer the challenges of the other person. It was a slightly weird but effective way of flushing stuff out for self-examination. In those conversations I sought to set myself on a clear path in life, to establish targets and attitudes and clear away emotional clutter: to decide, essentially, who I was and wanted to be. I was, in essence, inventing myself.

I decided I would have a family of my own and that my children would be the first in the family to go to university (which they were). I reaffirmed my intention to see the world as a foreign correspondent and decided I would live in India. Robert Clive, nawabs, maharajahs, the Battle of Plassey – these words romped around my head all the time. India seemed to be inside me.

I also made a decision that shaped everything that came after it – I decided to stop dragging around a weight of bitterness over the past and especially to stop feeling self-pity, because I didn't like being a miserable bugger feeling angry with the world. I had seen close-up what anger could do among relatives who waged feuds that ended only when the protagonists were dead, leaving a nasty smell of wasted life.

In order to fulfil that decision I needed to reach out to my parents and befriend them, which initially felt fake and awkward, because much of me wanted to stay angry, to cause hurt, to lash out with cruel words. But I reminded myself that I had never been hungry, unclothed or unsheltered and that my brother and I were indulged with generous presents come Christmas and birthdays. My parents were damaged, hard-working people struggling to pay the bills and get through a tough post-war life, and they did what they could with what little they had. My mother couldn't help being how she was because, I have no doubt, she was very seriously mentally ill. Perspective is everything.

Denied the oxygen of anger, the past steadily lost power over me. I phoned my parents once a week from wherever I was in the world, unless I was somewhere without phones. Those calls were important to me. Mastering the past was mastering the present, and by staying in touch I was tacitly reassuring my parents that the past was behind us so that they, too, could put it aside, because I knew a lot of what happened haunted them – especially my dad, at heart a good man.

He tried a few times to talk about the occasion he beat me with his fists, sending me crashing into that long mirror in the bedroom and leaving me spitting blood from a punch in the mouth. I was around 12. My mother had wound him up into this state with her forensic skills of manipulation. I picked myself up and goaded him to hit me again. He screamed that he would kill me if I didn't stop staring at him. I didn't cry, didn't move, but I looked away and my father walked off. A short while later he returned, sobbing and saying sorry, while my mother stood silently in the background.

What happened to him that day was an aberration, a one-off mega-explosion. That was not who he was. He was not a violently inclined person, merely a frustrated one plodding through life without levity or respite from the grind. He would very occasionally erupt when pushed too hard for too long, but never to the extent of that day. I would sometimes watch him staring aimlessly at the little black-and-white television waiting to go to work for the 10pm shift, sadness rising out of him as plain as the smoke from his roll-up cigarettes.

To understand him was to forgive him, and that was where I wanted to leave it when I grew up, but he seemed to be racked by the memory of that beating. I would never let him talk about it, however, and perhaps that was wrong, even cruel. I simply couldn't risk the damage it might do to us both to go back to that time, and to the relationship I had carefully built with him. Whenever I visited my parents, usually once a year after I started working abroad, my dad and I would go to the pub and talk about everything but past family life, and we had delightful times.

He talked a lot about the war, because it was the most interesting thing that happened to him. He was at the Falaise Gap, the decisive engagement of the Battle of Normandy – he drove big lorries – and told me lots of times how he took the wedding ring off a long-dead Jerry and the entire finger came away with it. He was made up to corporal but busted back to private for borrowing a tank transporter to visit my mother.

I never saw a scrap of affection between them. They never

touched, kissed or shared any of those fleeting gestures that might have suggested they loved each other. They never used each other's names. Both answered to 'mate.' My mother used to lock him out of their bedroom whenever she left the house because she didn't trust him to look after her little dog, and he would come home from shift work unable to go to bed until she got back. He would try picking the lock with a piece of wire, and sometimes succeeded. And of course the day came when he said 'fuck this' and shouldered the door open.

He was never called 'dad' by my brother or me. We never knew what to call him because 'dad' felt too intimate for somebody who was sometimes within sight but never quite within reach, until one day my brother started calling him Pappy. I adopted it, too, because its sarcastic tone felt right. Neither of us had a name for my mother, though. She didn't qualify for 'mum', so it was 'excuse me' or a tap on the shoulder to draw her attention.

My brother again came to the rescue when he started calling her 'Pussyfoot' as a sort of mockery, and it stuck. She answered to it because it was better than nothing. She sometimes tried to get us to call her 'mum', but we just couldn't. Later on I managed to begin 'Dear Mum' in letters to her from abroad but it felt clumsy, too late and just plain awkward.

I was in Haiti covering a civil uprising in 1986 when the foreign editor of *The Times* (I had been working there for several years) called to tell me my father had died. The content of that call, its gravity emphasised by a tremolo in the voice of the crosspatch who made it, did not immediately register. I was still reeling from something quite inconsequential in context but gruesome nevertheless – I had been to a cockfight, a popular atrocity in Haiti, when poor men in rags screamed and raged as cockerels tore each other apart, a leg here, an eye there, feathers flying, blood spitting, sharpened claws sinking deep into each other, whole wings torn off and sent spinning across the room. The cacophony was ear-splitting as money changed hands right to the end, when one of the cocks keeled over dead. The room was thick with cigarette smoke. Little bottles of cheap liquor fuelled the mania.

I had gone for colour and background to the Haiti story and it jolted me. The violence was grotesque. Blood had splashed over my face and clothes because I was right by the cockpit, and the peculiar instinct of every victorious cock to stand on the corpse of its rival and crow its head off was somehow an obscenity too much. Not that it crowed for long: every winner had its neck wrung, because no cock was fit to fight twice. I was not long back in my hotel room when the call came through from London to tell me about my dad, and I was too shaken to make much sense of it.

'Don't bother to file, go home.' Those were the words of the foreign editor. What a horrible task to befall him. I must have sounded indifferent, because my emotions simply couldn't engage with it. Despite being told not to, I insisted on dictating that day's story to *The Times* copytakers, reading it off my notepad and amending it as I went along, as was my practice. Then, still not fully registering what I had been told, I began to figure out how to get out of Haiti, which by now had exploded in a rampage of anarchy. Gangs were roaming the streets of Port au Prince, the capital, smashing everything that could be smashed, burning cars and beating people half to death. It was one of those poverty-induced random explosions for which Haiti was renowned, and it was perilous to go outside the secured precincts of the hotel.

Finally I found somebody who, for lots of dollars, agreed to try to take me to the airport. I had no idea if any flights were leaving because communications with the airport were down. What a journey that was, squealing around burning barricades, dodging bricks that were hurled at us and charging straight at marauding gangs and hoping they weren't armed. We made it nevertheless, and the driver went off to stay somewhere in the countryside. I caught the absolutely last flight out before the airport was closed, and it happened to be going to New York. I caught an instant connection from there to London. I never travelled with more than carry-on luggage, which made that possible.

I reached the nearest railway station to my parents' house – it was Stanford-le-Hope – in a jet-lagged daze. From civil war in Haiti I was now back to the familiar streets of my childhood and all the memories of my time tramping them as a reporter for the local weekly newspaper, the *Essex and Thurrock Gazette*, where I had started my working life as a tea-boy before they let me train as a reporter.

I bought *The Times* at the railway station kiosk and there was my story, top of the page with my by-line and a Haiti dateline. It was the oddest experience to be in two places at once. My father had died here in Essex and I was covering civil strife in Haiti because it said so in the paper. I walked around to gather myself, reminding myself why I was here and not there. It was not quite dawn and the streets were still. The silence held me: I felt its peace and didn't want it to end. I walked around until daylight, then took a taxi from the railway station to the house, a pebble-dashed bungalow at the end of a cul-de-sac where I had grown up from the age of five. Everything was both familiar and strange.

My mother was sleeping on a sofa. She looked small, broken and vulnerable, and in that moment I promised myself that I would be her guardian. Although I had reached an accommodation with the past, I knew I would always feel the damage, always feel a bit of an outsider; that I would never quite fit anywhere; this I accepted as the manageable and not exceptional legacy of an upbringing that most of the world's children would have been glad of. But from the moment of promising myself to care for my mother I truly became free. I had the sensation of an ending and a beginning. I was 40.

I look back on my mother's life with great pity for her. She never owned a passport, never flew in a plane nor saw a palm tree (a lifelong wish), never knew a thing about the world beyond her own, never knew much love, never had much money, never read a novel, never had a spoil beyond a week or two in a rented caravan or a down-market boarding house. The only tender touch she remembered receiving from her father, she used to say, was when she fell and broke her leg as a little girl and he carried her indoors. And her mother, my Gran Ockendon, wasn't given to soft stuff.

My mother lived to 92 and was healthy until her mid-80s despite frequently going on extreme diets and vitamin-pill binges rather than eat. Being thin was an obsession. I think she was a lifetime intermittent anorexic. She turned out to be a fine grandmother to my three children – a recessive oddball, yes, and prone to spiteful behaviour like hiding their passports, reading their diaries and telling them lies about each other, but she was always glad to see them in her particular way.

My two girls attended boarding school more than an hour's drive from her house, and she never failed to collect them and give them a weekend away in her bungalow when they asked for it. They would go back with a bag of goodies each, and right there on the front seat of her small Ford would sit her latest poodle or Chihuahua in its blanket-lined basket, with the grandchildren consigned to the back seat, giggling with the absurdity of it.

CHAPTER TWO

Gran Brown was a mystery, and not only because she read books. She was of another hue, different from us, her manner suggesting a faded but unmistakable touch of the posh. She bore no false airs or pretentions: she was naturally and irredeemably different, and even her voice carried markers of a different order.

It was weird seeing her with her son David, my father. They were like different species, this solidly working-class bloke and this refined woman with gravitas and a gentle air of authority. When she was around my mother it could have been the Queen trying to find common ground with an intimidated scullery maid. Both were earnest in their dislike of each other.

Gran always bought me books for Christmas. For my birthday she baked a pile of what she called Welsh cakes – dry, round little things that I loved because they were especially for me. She spent the last years of her life alone in a pensioner's cottage in Corringham and was a frequent sight in the local library. I tried several times to draw her into her past, but she wouldn't give much away.

A family member discovered she had been well schooled for a while when very young, courtesy of the Earl of Dudley, whose illegitimate daughter she may have been. The earl's largesse died with him, but the early education left its mark. She married a solidly middle-class man, a master stonemason who carved gargoyles out of slabs of rock and was paid handsomely for his art. This was my dad's father, but he died of TB when my dad was five. Gran had to take in washing and later married a ditch-digger who never said anything much longer than a grunt. He was known as Pop.

They lived in a grubby town called Dowlais, outside Merthyr Tydfil, which mainly comprised arrow-straight rows of tiny terraced houses built for coal miners. Pop walked from Wales to Essex to find work, which is why they moved to Corringham when my dad and his brother Bill were still little. They were poor: my dad would be sent out to collect stinging nettles to be boiled and served with dinner. They rented successive properties over the years and ended up late in life in a rundown cottage on the River Thames marshes by the Shell oil refinery, and for years they had neither gas nor electricity.

The only access was down a muddy tractor track with a gate across it to stop farm animals getting out. Lighting came from kerosene lamps, heating from coal fires. Goats and sheep ceaselessly attacked their vegetable garden and

Gran was always charging at them with a broom. I loved going there. It was a wide-open playground, with nothing nearby save for the oil refinery with its big eternal flame atop a tall chimney to burn off waste gas. I grew up with that flame. Corringham and its flame seemed inseparable. It's gone now, along with the refinery itself.

Pop had one of those faces and moustaches you see in old photos from the horse-and-cart era. I used to stare at one of his gnarled old hands because the tip of a little finger was missing. According to family legend he half chopped it off in an accident while digging a ditch, yanked it off and carried on digging. I have no recollection of him ever saying a single word to me about anything, ever. My dad had a hard time growing up under Pop's charge, although he would never talk in detail about it, and somewhere within that relationship, I suspect, lay the answer to his suppressed and unhappy nature.

My mother controlled the family finances (there were always cash-filled envelopes in the cupboard marked 'gas', 'electric', 'water', 'hire purchase', etc) and decided I should attend a private school – yes indeed – called Clark's College, which was crammed into a rundown pre-Victorian house in Southend-on-Sea and turned out to be a dump both as an alleged school and as a building. It was damp, draughty and visibly falling down. It had maybe a dozen 'teachers,' none of whom could produce proof of training whenever a disgruntled parent asked for it. It was a preposterous con. How it got licensed to operate (if it ever did) is anybody's guess. Perhaps by claiming to be 'private' it escaped the rules. The 'teachers' were mostly drawn out of retirement from careers totally unrelated to teaching. Mr White, the headmaster, seemed older than the building and wore spats. In the 1960s! He banned the use of biros and fountain pens, forcing us to dip pen-nibs into pots of cheap ink that ran all over the page.

One man nominally taught every subject I took in that non-school save for shorthand and typing, but he knew next to nothing about any of them and so spent every lesson prattling about irrelevant stuff until the bell went. Sometimes he would spend a lesson reading out entire sections from textbooks as a gesture to teaching something, albeit vicariously. His name was Mr Timcke, a miserable, dyspeptic old blatherskite with a shiny bald head and a massive hump on his back that forced him to walk stooped over as if looking for something. He must have been close to 80.

I spent three years at this place from the age of 13 without receiving a single lesson in anything relevant, bar shorthand. I received not one lesson in history, mathematics, literature, geography, religious affairs or science. The main subject headings apart from shorthand and typing were Commercial Geography (want to know the routes of commercial shipping?), Accountancy, Bookkeeping and Handwriting.

Mr Timcke was amazed when I passed the GCE English examination because he hadn't given a single lesson to prepare me for it, and wouldn't have been able to anyway. He told the entire class in front of me, 'If he can pass it, anyone can.' I had studied for it by myself with books from the public library, believing it would help me into journalism.

After three years I left that dreadful institution aged 16 with one O-level, a certificate for shorthand and another for typing. I had a bizarre flare for shorthand and was top not only of my class but almost of all England, reaching 160 wpm. To my unsuspecting parents I was now an intellectual. My father started deferring to me with questions about things he didn't understand and if he had to write a letter he would ask me to do it for him. It was all very surreal.

My class had about 30 girls and a token number of boys with parents as gullible as my own who thought we were getting a normal education, and because of the demographics, all my friends bar one were female. Carol, Stephanie, Margaret, Maureen and Norma: how lovely you were. Norma is still my friend. We've clocked up 60 years so far. She's lived up north for decades and now talks funny.

My parents never did realise what kind of school it was, but it meant I wore a uniform and impressed the neighbours. At one point Mr White threatened to expel me because I adamantly refused to wear a school cap, but he backed down when I didn't. I disposed of it by chucking it onto the platform of a passing bus. My father worried that something wasn't quite right with me when I asked if I could have a typewriter for Christmas when I was 16, the year I left school, because I thought it would be useful if I ever became a journalist – although he wouldn't have known about that. What with the typewriter, the shorthand, and always being in the company of girls, I think he was worried about my manhood. My brother was into judo (he became a black belt), so he was OK with him. He saw me as a bit effete.

It was an hour's commute on the bus to get to this so-called school. It was a joyful journey because there were three of us on it every day from Corringham and we were great mates – the above-mentioned Norma, Dangle and me. Dangle was Jean François Pierre D'Angelis, who became Dangle courtesy of a teacher who couldn't pronounce that mouthful. Unsurprisingly his father was French, and had fled to England to escape justice for nefarious deeds back home.

We always occupied the three-seater bench at the back of the Number Two bus upstairs, where Dangle and I competed for the attentions of Norma and tickled her divine knees. I was the first to get an innocent little kiss, and felt like Caesar. Dangle became a bread delivery driver, a milkman and finally a lorry driver, and lived in Mansfield, where he bolstered the fortunes of a pub called The Bridge.

Clark's College – what clever bastard gave it that imposing name? – was essentially a place for training girls to be shorthand-typists, but it did at least hand me a lifetime's gift when it taught me shorthand. Actually it didn't really teach it to me so much as introduce me to it, because when I realised it could further my journalistic ambitions I worked hard at it. I took down BBC radio news bulletins to build up my speed and devoured a monthly teach-yourself-shorthand magazine called Pitman's Bulletin.

Shorthand was not only decisive in getting me into jour-nalism in the first place; years later it was decisive in getting me into *The Times*. I would rather have achieved those feats by people thinking I had the makings of a journalist, but never mind. Clark's so-called College was a curate's egg, much as I'd prefer to say that every bit of it was a total waste.

So when I wrote to *The Southend Standard* asking if they had a job, I was able to offer super-fast shorthand and an English O-level. Ken Broadley, the editor-in-chief, invited me to an interview. The paper was then a grand old weekly with a whopping circulation of 70,000.

I sat in the interview waiting room with a dozen others. I was useless at the interview, utterly tongue-tied, even though it only lasted a matter of minutes. So lad, why do you want to join *The Southend Standard?* I had absolutely no idea, at least none I could articulate, so I nodded and grinned and shuffled and mumbled. Things were going so badly I decided right there and then to change tack and announce that I wanted to be a photographer. I hadn't thought of that before. Mr Broadley dismissed that straight away because there was no vacancy. 'Anyway, lad, with that shorthand you'll be a reporter on this paper if you're anything.' And so I slipped away, certain of rejection.

A week later a letter arrived saying I had got the job. It said so right there, on headed notepaper, two paragraphs long, with Mr Broadley's signature on it and a sentence that began, 'I am pleased to inform you...' Shorthand had cracked it for me. I danced in front of the mirror and said over and over, 'I'm a journalist. I'm a journalist.' And I would get six pounds ten shillings a week in wages, not much less than my father was earning. Not only that, in time they gave me a little expense account to put petrol in my moped. That felt swank.

Mr Broadley came to regret his decision. I showed so little promise he tried to coax me into not completing my six-month trial period, which he extended to 12 months when I refused to quit. I never stopped posing in front of that mirror, never lost the ravening hunger or the pin-sharp focus – never doubted that somehow I would become a reporter. I didn't know I was supposed to give up.

It wasn't really fair of Ken Broadley to try to fire me, because the first nine months of my 'journalistic career' were spent making tea and running errands, so my attempts to write stories were always a flop because nobody bothered to show me how. I was paralysed by shyness and found it difficult to relate to the reporters in the office, who all said 'cheers' instead of goodnight, spoke with great familiarity among themselves and pretty much ignored me. They all seemed so clever and informed: half a dozen wiseacres to one trembling galoot almost too intimidated to talk out loud.

Nine months of making tea and errand-running, every working day of it, didn't dim the flame. The bottom line was that I was working in a newspaper, watching and learning, and I had no intention of letting go without a fight. In the end Mr Broadley grudgingly agreed to my being indentured for three years. He told me I had him 'over a barrel' because I seemed so determined, and although I had no idea what that expression meant I suspected it wasn't a compliment.

My father came to the office to sign the indenture because I was under-age, and looked terrified in such surroundings.

Three times a day I had to run to the railway station with a parcel full of typewritten copy generated by the reporters and have it sent to the printers in Southend-on-Sea. I had been assigned to *The Southend Standard's* sister paper in Grays, the aforementioned *Essex and Thurrock Gazette*, later shortened to the *Thurrock Gazette*. It was set in the heart of smokestack industries that made cement and a host of other polluting products that covered the town in dust and stench. Grays deserved its name.

I made tea as often as summoned to do so, because I knew my survival was precarious. Besides making tea and running to the station with bulging packets marked 'News Intelligence' (how romantic that sounded; it felt grand to be transporting the words that thousands of people would be reading come Friday) I would be dispatched to collect cigarettes, sandwiches, bottles of drink, and anything else anybody wanted, including fish and chips, pork pie and chips, sausages and chips or just chips, plenty of vinegar and salt, old chap. Learning how to write a story? Dream on. Nobody had the inclination to trouble with that, and besides they were mostly novices themselves.

The chief reporter was a foppish dandy called Simon Bradley, who used some device he kept in a drawer to straighten his curly hair before gluing it into a meticulous coiffure with a brutal dose of hairspray. He always did this seated before a large mirror on his desk, and this theatre of public pampering evidently gave him some weird pleasure.

He was a social climber who joined the Thurrock Rotary Club and used to tell us derogatory stories about the dullards he met there. He was fond of placing one of the reporters, a gamine little blonde in her mid-twenties, on his knee and bouncing her about, which she didn't mind at all because she was an easy-going sort of woman. She enjoyed regaling us with graphic and sometimes shocking tales of amatory adventures with various studs and swains – including a local town councillor, whose impotence she tried valiantly, but vainly, to cure – until, without warning, she stumbled into marriage and monogamy. I shall call her Mary.

One joyous day Simon announced that I could accompany her to the Thurrock Council Road Safety Committee meeting that evening and return with her to the office that night to watch her write it up. It was the first crack in their armour. They were going to let me train.

Soon after this a teenager called Phyllis joined the paper as a trainee and became my first real girlfriend. She had disturbing religious inclinations and years later married a missionary and moved to Africa. There wasn't a joke in the world about philistines or syphilis that she hadn't endured in the playgrounds of her childhood, and she seemed hardened by it. She projected a quite terrifying and slightly belligerent self-confidence. It turned out that she had gone to Palmers, no less, and claimed ownership of several A-levels, and here she was, destined to go out with this lumprenprole.

On our first date I discussed with her the first grown-up book I ever completed. It was *Allan Quartermain*, which I had found by chance in the local library when I was around

14, having decided that I should try my hand at this reading lark so I might stop feeling less like a complete lunkhead. Phyllis knew it of course, and it was exciting to discuss it with her: my first ever conversation of that kind. What a book that was to stir a rampant young imagination. I read it over and over during an entire school summer holiday and dreamed of being out there in wild Africa alongside Umslopogaas and not stuck in this dull bungalow. I contentedly spent that summer holiday mostly by myself, reading or out cycling or tramping through the woods on One Tree Hill, my head full of that magnificent book. Solitude is a faithful friend if you don't fear it.

Phyllis plunged into training as a reporter without having to make tea, which struck me as unfair but there you go: she was a Palmers girl after all. I had by then been released from tea-making by the arrival of a new peon-cum-wannabe reporter, a gangling chap called George who flicked his head every few seconds as if he had a nervous tic, but he was only shaking his hair out of his face. He had terrible acne, which made me feel better about mine.

After my liberation from the teapot I got in everybody's way by looking over their shoulders as they wrote their stories and listening obtrusively to their telephone conversations. I went into the office secretly late at night and sat at my typewriter (the one I got at Christmas when I was 16, and which I still possess) copying out articles from *The Daily Telegraph* to try to get the feel of how to construct a sentence, if not a paragraph and, Heaven forfend, a story. I had never heard of a split infinitive, but through this exercise I came to understand one when I saw it, even if I couldn't explain it. I learned to understand the difference between insurance and assurance, uninterested and disinterested, and little delicacies like that. Over time I began to feel the rhythm of telling a tale, be it a serious story or something light-hearted. I tried copying out the columnists, but they were too clever by half and used vocabulary that flummoxed me.

I sometimes stayed in the office half the night copying out the entire front page of the *Telegraph* and reading the words back to myself very slowly to try to understand how to write sparingly and save a word or two by moving a sentence around. I did this for a good couple of years. Sometimes a policeman would bang on the office door to find out who was in there in the middle of the night.

There was a man at the paper who had a university degree and whose pastime was doing clause analysis. He would take a complex sentence and dissect it into its constituent parts – for fun. His name was Cliff Longley and he could have drunk all the tea in India. He never left me alone, albeit with great courtesy, during my tea-making days. 'Chris... tea? Thanks so much.' And he smoked furiously. Out to collect his fags, into the kitchen to make more tea, down to the railway station with a parcel of news, more tea for Cliff: a servant to the savant.

I accompanied Mary on lots of stories and watched with not a little wonderment how she went about doing interviews, always with a clear idea of what she was after, then bashing it out on the typewriter so fluently that she might have been copying it out from somewhere – at least, so it seemed to me at the time. I was still not being sent out on stories by myself on the perfectly reasonable grounds that I was not fit to be let loose. They gave me hand-written reports sent in from Toc-H (whoever they were), the Women's Institute, Thurrock Spastics' Society and such-like to turn into readable English, usually to the consternation of the authors (sometimes a vicar trying his hand at literary flourishes) who preferred their own versions. My frustration was ready to explode. I wanted to be a proper reporter, dammit.

Come lunchtime it was my task to answer the phones while the grown-ups went to the pub – or, more usually, the nearby Oddfellows Club, because the beer was cheaper and it did good sandwiches. Should any news unusually break surface I was to call them. One lunchtime a policeman phoned to inform us that a lorry had hit a railway bridge and its load had fallen onto a car and trapped the driver and his son inside. I rang the Oddfellows Club, but hung up before it answered. Sod it. They won't give me stories to do so I'll damn well grab one. I bestrode my moped and attended the accident, getting the names, talking to the police and even to the car driver who was still trapped but miraculously unhurt, as was his son. They were cut out by the fire brigade.

You have never seen a madder collection of people when I walked into the office with a notebook full of this stuff. Simon, the chief reporter, raged at me and demanded that I read it all out so he could write it up, but I refused.

I wrote the story all by myself, terribly so, and it was thoroughly re-written, but it was the nearest I had come to that glorious sensation of seeing something in the paper with a headline on it and knowing that it was there because I sort of put it there.

They let me off the leash after that to do some footling little stories without ever leaving the office, until my real break came when they sent me off to interview a new curate at the Tilbury Seaman's Mission. I went with David Henderson, the photographer, on the back of his Lambretta, crash-helmet free, whizzing round the bends and roundabouts like a free man sailing the oceans, out there in the air while millions laboured in offices and factories, and here was I – a reporter, out on a job. Oh bliss. My first official assignment.

The curate was very sweet and David snapped away at him with his great big camera, ostentatiously erecting a tripod with a white sheet on it to reflect the light, which I thought was all a bit much for a simple head-and-shoulders shot. I tore into the curate as I thought I should, having seen on television how it was done. I demanded to know what changes he would implement. 'Oh I think it's all going along quite well as it is,' he said, or words to that effect, and I wrote something withering in my notebook. 'So, no changes,' I said contemptuously out loud.

It went on in that vein and I left him, I thought, suitably unsettled. When I got back to the office to try to write up the story I discovered I had omitted to ask his age or whether he was married, so I had to ring him up. He was very nice about it but I think I heard a snort at my expense. Come Friday there it was, my story, nothing but a caption beneath the picture but nevertheless all my own, not with my name on it but right there in the paper for the world – well, OK, quite a lot of people – to see. I read those 100 words over and over.

Next up, golden weddings, lots of them. Once or twice, diamond weddings. Dangerous potholes in the road. Vandalised phone boxes. Speeding traffic and somebody's going to get killed one day if they don't do something about it. Flower shows. Retirements. Agricultural shows. The Road Safety Committee. I have no interest in football, but I was sent to cover a football match, and had no idea at the end of it what the score was. I called the club to find out, pretending to be a fan, and asked who had scored for the home side. I plagiarised a football report from the *Daily Express* and substituted all the names. It had phrases like 'slammed the ball into the net' and 'pounded the leather with a powerful right.' I was never sent to cover another football match, so I presume I was rumbled.

It wasn't long before a ghastly aspect of the job of a local newspaper reporter confronted me. A young man had died in a road accident and I went to see the grieving family to solicit a photograph of him. I could feel the grief as I stood there on the doorstep, invasive, in the wrong place, feeling like a bastard. 'I am sorry to disturb you at such a time but I wonder if you have a photograph of your son I could use for the paper?'

I was facing the grief-racked mother, whose face folded

into something of a smile. She invited me in and seemed to take pleasure rummaging around her photo albums for a nice picture of her boy, who I think was in his early teens. Dad looked on, glum, silent, but not hostile. The curtains were closed. Various shadows of other people moved silently around but I deliberately didn't register them.

I couldn't understand it. The intrusion was almost welcome. Their boy was to be in the paper, probably on page one, and after I had performed this task on various occasions I understood how grief is so individual it can go a dozen different ways. Some would welcome you, some would get angry, others would just stand there limply, not knowing what to say. There came a time when I resolutely refused to perform this awful task again after doing something utterly awful. A family gave me their only photograph of a dead relative, a road accident victim, and I lost it after it was published and had been properly returned to me from the printers. It just vanished out of my desk, spirited away in the night, carried off by ghosts.

I steeled myself to confess to the family, who had emphasised repeatedly that it was their only photograph. I stood at their front door and grovelled with apologies. They were wonderful about it and said I had written a nice article. Why didn't they scream, call the paper and demand I be sacked?

After perhaps two years into my three-year indenture I started to feel a bit like a reporter. It certainly felt a long way from July 29, 1963, my first day of work. I remember the feelings of that day: out of depth, out of all familiarity, listening to words like 'copy' and 'NIB' and 'fudge' and feeling

I had landed in Greece speaking Turkish. NIB? It came to me before the day was out. News In Brief. The fudge was the little space reserved on the front page for late-breaking news, officially known as Stop Press. They used to have to come up with late-breaking news to fill up that irritating slot. 'Fire brigade called to grass fire at recreation ground' was a typical last resort. I was now part of this world. At least I had the vocabulary.

The reporter on the *Gazette* who most impressed me was called Bert. He was quite the lady's man with a great big Elvis quiff and the contrived air of a bored old newspaperman. I watched him typing up a story about some local kid who got marooned on a railway station in Spain because his parents thought he was already on the train. Somehow the story reached Bert. He wrote: 'Jimmy stood alone on the platform as the minutes ticked by on the station clock...' I asked Bert how he knew the station had a clock because he had never been there – or had he? He looked at me patronisingly and said it was a reasonable assumption that the station had a clock and that it was ticking. This was what he called 'colour' to give a story a little oomph. 'Like giving it some atmosphere,' I offered. 'Colour,' he snapped. That was the word for red-blooded reporters.

One of my first observations at the paper was how people spoke. My language was the demotic of my parents, who would have tea when really it was dinner and dinner when it was lunch and said 'what he done' and 'you was' with an accent that was a chip off the Cockney block. Here, in this island of people with O- and A-levels, the accent wasn't posh but it wasn't raw like mine, and I steadily and unconsciously adopted it. I fretted constantly about my appalling education and crammed my head with all manner of stuff from library books, and little by little I started to feel less of an imposter. Step by tiny step, I was moving towards the dream.

CHAPTER THREE

Simon stopped bouncing Mary on his knee, called me to his cubicle in the newsroom and assumed a serious face. Mary gave me a wink as she walked out, which rather confounded me. Simon announced that he was giving me a 'beat.' This would mean covering certain assigned towns from which I would be expected to extract lots of stories every week, and those towns were Corringham and Stanford-le-Hope. I was to be an observer of my home turf, an insider with an outsider's eyes. I pumped Simon's hand in joyful thanks, and his face assumed its default smile. Mary scurried in and gave me a congratulatory hug, because the news had already been whispered into her ear.

I turned in stories that hardly shook the world but which resonated in a local newspaper. I got to know local councillors and activists, business owners, church ministers, head teachers – anybody likely to steer me to a story. The freedom was wonderful. Sometimes I wouldn't go into the office for days, except at night to write up my stuff and leave it on Simon's desk. I was a child of the sixties but never engaged much with them, save for attending smoky folk clubs in the back-rooms of pubs on Saturday nights. My world was finding news.

There were stories everywhere. There was the pigeon fancier with a bird that came home after eight months, the darts player who won a regional prize, the gardener with a monstrous marrow gracing his allotment, the fisherman who caught a whopper, the golfer who got his second hole-in-one after 30 years. I wrote about a man with a huge sunflower in his garden and people starting writing in to say they had a bigger one, and before I knew it a competition was under way that lasted as long as the sunflowers did. It was meat and gravy for a local paper.

And I got a real scoop. The professional heavyweight boxer Billy Walker mysteriously owned a petrol station in Corringham called Punch Petrol, and I heard that both he and his brother George sometimes occupied the flat upstairs (which was another mystery). So on the off-chance I climbed the concrete steps on the side of the building and knocked at the door, and George answered.

'What?' he said.

'Hello, I'm from the local paper...'

He was menacing, a real East End bruiser, big and gruff. But he invited me in and I looked around with amazement. Weren't these people rich? There was a formica-topped table with dirty coffee cups all over it, torn lino on the floor, strip lighting and a sink full of unwashed crockery. What were they doing in such a place? I never did figure that out, any more than I could figure out why they would want to run a petrol station with a naff name in humble old Corringham. Billy had bought the former Church of England rectory nearby in Fobbing and set up a gymnasium there, and I asked if I could see it and watch him train. George said Billy would show me around but I wouldn't be allowed to watch him train. An appointment was made. Billy didn't talk much. That was George's job.

David, the photographer, turned up at the forecourt of Punch Petrol in his little Austin A40. I climbed into the back and Billy got into the front, and the wheels on the other side practically lifted off the ground. His shoulders were so wide he pressed David against the door so he had to drive with one arm out the window. It was a wonder that the car, with its sewing machine-sized engine, got up the hill to the old rectory. Billy showed me around as David snapped away. The story got a big show and it was a landmark for me because it had my by-line on it. That felt like a starter gun.

If you want a peaceful life on a local paper you must be sedulously accurate. If you say a man won a prize for the biggest tomato and it was a carrot, look out when he meets you in the street. Being a local reporter was always the traditional route to bigger newspapers, and to my mind this system produced a better crop of hacks than those emerging from Media Studies at university and running BBC News five minutes later.

The stories I turned in were wildly varied. I heard about

a young dancer who performed in the Black and White Minstrel Show, a ragingly offensive and hugely popular show that ran for 20 years on the BBC, and she wore something just shy of naked for our photographer. There was a terrific pub singer who was confident about getting a recording contract and becoming famous (but never did). There were always retirements to report, when a wan-looking Mr Johnson or Mr Jacobs received a patronising speech from the youthful boss thanking him for 43 years' service.

I would read church notice boards and attend working men's clubs in the hope of finding a tale. I got to know lots of publicans and urged them to keep ears and eyes open for me, and occasionally one would come up with something. My own mother gave me a cracking story that was followed up by the London *Evening Standard*, concerning a woman she worked with at the Bata shoe factory. This woman was from Riga in Latvia and she had fled to England before the war. She was now going to risk returning to see her dying father. She had a husband and children in Corringham who she might never see again if the communist government wouldn't let her back. What a choice, what a gamble, what a story.

I was pleased with my article until I read the *Evening Standard* version. They had interviewed her and did it ten times better, conveying the fear and pathos while all I had done was tell it straight, without mood. Dare I say it – without colour. Like Bert with his imagined station clock, the *Evening Standard* reporter brought the story alive. It taught me that I had far to go. The woman returned home after a month away, without incident, but I felt too demor-alised to want to report it.

I attended Sunday church services in the hope of hearing a newsworthy sermon, which I never did. I suppose the vicars were a bit wary when they saw a reporter in the back pew brandishing a notebook. I saw headmasters, too, but could never bring myself to see the head at Hassenbrook. That would have felt a bit too weird. But on a couple of occasions I waited outside the school gate to watch the kids coming out to see if I could see an image of myself in them, and found in many of their faces the same doubts, the inbred inferiority, the second-rate feeling. So many of them seemed languid and tired, as if defeat already weighed on them.

After a few delightful years patrolling Corringham and Stanford-le-Hope I had a major breakthrough. The paper had what was called a 'slip-edition' in which two pages, the front page and one other, were devoted to news from the Thames-side town of Rainham on the outskirts of east London. The reporter in charge had quit, and I was appointed in his place by Ken Broadley himself. He said he'd changed his opinion of me. That was a big moment.

Rainham was juicy as a peach. Big bad things happened in a ceaseless swirl of crime, social deprivation, drink, drugs and all the ills that broken society gorges on, all of which was enhanced by an ever-present stench of smoke and chemicals from its polluting industries. And it was downright ugly.

I introduced a feature called *Down Your Road* in which I banged on doors and asked to intrude on people's lives. 'Hello, I'm from the *Rainham Gazette* and I'm doing a series of articles about people who live in this street.' Every week I profiled four or five families in a randomly chosen street and was amazed at how many good stories hid behind ordinary front doors.

People were remarkably willing – indeed anxious – to talk about themselves. Once I got out my notebook and started asking questions they would reveal intimate stuff about their childhoods, marriages and bereavements, their disappointments and dreams, but I was always careful never to write anything that might embarrass them. A faith healer was the spookiest character I encountered. He seemed to see deep into me. I challenged him to remove a small mark that had always been on my hand: it was gone next day and never came back.

There was a development of high-rise council flats called Mardyke Flats that were infested with vandals and drug dealers, and I knocked on doors with an uncommon lack of success because people were afraid to open them. I thought that whoever designed those places should be forced to live in them. The few people who did let me in talked about isolation, yobs and warring neighbours. I couldn't think of a worse fate than being old and alone in such a building in such a town.

I built up the *Rainham Gazette* from two pages to four most weeks, working flat-out and loving it, and the circulation went way up. I even started doing reviews from the Queen's Theatre in Hornchurch, which sent complimentary tickets for its plays: that felt really posh. On Mondays my first call was always to the vicarage, where five vicars from

Rainham and surrounding parishes gathered to share notes and ideas about the coming week. I timed it to coincide with their tea break and usually came away with something to work on.

The *Rainham Gazette* was doing well enough to justify assigning another reporter to it, and that reporter was, to my abiding joy, my girlfriend Phyllis. I was now her boss. Huh! Around this time a councillor I knew arranged for me to meet the news editor of a national newspaper, the *Daily Sketch* – RIP – with a view to my getting a job there. I was to meet him in a pub in Hornchurch one Saturday lunchtime. I arrived early and worked myself into a complete lather at the thought of meeting a real live Fleet Street news editor. When he arrived I had to rush to the loo to be sick. He probably thought I was drunk. He never offered me a job, thank God, because it was an awful rag and doomed to fold.

My three-year indenture, conducted under the auspices of the National Council for the Training of Journalists, meant going to college every Friday in Plaistow in London's East End to be taught things like libel law. Much of the course was devoted to shorthand, so I'd slip away for a matinee film somewhere. At the end of three years I received a diploma saying I was a qualified journalist. I read it over and over. I had made it. Now anything was possible. The *Gazette* hadn't given up on me, and for that I thanked Ken Broadley. He didn't seem surprised when, a few months later, I resigned. 'Good luck, lad,' was all he said.

I went to France to work for a certain Dr Coronat, a

medical doctor, who was crippled by arthritis and lived in a wheelchair in a grand house in Arcachon, near Bordeaux, with a very angry wife and a live-in carer who was about to leave him. I was the new carer. My job was to help him onto the toilet, put him to bed, shave him and run his errands. The point of this was to learn French. One had to speak languages to be a foreign correspondent, right?

Dr Coronat had every right to be a bastard, which he was, always yelling, snapping, trying to lash out with his crippled hands, always terrified that I would lose control of him during his wheelchair outings and utterly baffled why I couldn't get 'à droite' and 'à gauche' round the right way. I did in the end, but we were enemies by then. He fired me after some months and I took a train to the south of France with little more French than I had started with, and eventually returned to England via a spell mucking around in Paris.

When I got home, jobless and skint, Phyllis was still waiting for me. I felt awfully worldly, this revenant returning from far away. I grabbed the Writers' and Artists' Year Book and wrote letters to dozens of papers asking for a job, and two replied. One was the *South Wales Argus*, which summoned me for an interview in which I was again thoroughly useless, and I never heard from them again. The second was for a job at the *Salisbury Journal*, another weekly when what I really wanted was a regional daily, but I would have taken anything.

The editor mentioned that they were opening up a new newspaper to be called the *Wimborne Journal* in Dorset.

Of course I would be too young to be in charge of such a project, but maybe I would like to be associated with it? Damn it, no, I didn't want to be associated with it, I wanted to run it, and suddenly I was all fire and confidence and raging with enthusiasm. I told him about *Down Your Road* and what I had done with the *Rainham Gazette* and ended up getting the job. Me, in charge of a whole newspaper! Well, OK, a newspaper that didn't exist, but it was wonderful and thrilling, especially at the age of 20.

I spent a week living above a pub in Salisbury as plans for the paper took shape and I searched for permanent accommodation. For a while I moved in with one of the sub-editors at the *Salisbury Journal*, a quiet bachelor who was glad of a little income from a lodger. Eventually I rented a caravan on a site called Sandy Balls (truly) in Ringwood, and set about gathering news for this impending publication.

The paper duly came out and the first front-page splash in it, carved out of my imagination, resonated with my past because it was about a railway bridge that some lorry was going to hit some day and shed its load and kill somebody if they didn't lower the road or raise the bridge. I had no idea if any of that was true, but the council came and dug out the road to increase the height of the bridge, just in case. I wrote all that first edition myself, and thereafter two assistants were sent along. What I discovered very quickly was that I was no manager of people. I had no idea how to delegate, for the simple reason that I didn't want to. While I worked they spent much of their time pulling trout from the stream

56

at the end of the garden at the back of the office. I didn't want them interfering with my paper.

I had my first foreign assignment on that little paper. Wimborne was twinned with Valognes in France and off I went with a delegation from the council, mayor and all, to be received with great ceremony over there. Gosh, oh my. I could smell it now, the thrill of being sent abroad. Foreign correspondent, war correspondent... We went over and back by ferry and I remember having the devil of a job writing up the report. Feature writing was still a challenge.

The *Coventry Evening Telegraph* wrote to me out of the blue in answer to a letter sent months earlier and invited me to an interview for a job that for some reason I got, despite my usual incompetence at the interview. I quickly engineered myself into the position of an off-diary reporter by not being in the office when I should have been but usually turning up with a story.

The *Telegraph* taught me about deadlines. The deadline for the first edition was at noon and there were four more editions until the Final at 5pm, and if you were writing a story with a 2pm deadline there was no point submitting it at 2.01pm because you would create chaos as they scrambled to assemble something in its place. This discipline taught me to write fast, to deliver on time and, extremely important, to write on length. No point getting a story in on time if it was 300 words too long and they had to waste ten minutes editing it down.

I did a series of articles entitled 'A Day In the Life Of,' in which I worked at other people's jobs. I did a shift as a dustman and emptied garbage all over people's lawns because back then dustmen lifted bins onto their shoulders, which was tougher than it looked. I worked down a coal mine, laboured on a building site and delivered milk at dawn.

The coal-mine experience hit me. Why would anybody even consider such a life? A metal 'cage' – that's what they called it – took us a mile into the ground, 20 of us packed tight against each other, some holding the bars like prisoners being escorted to the gulag. A clattering system of chains and pulleys lowered us slowly down and ten minutes later we bounced to a clanking stop. I followed the men down a long black corridor illuminated only by our helmet lamps before we fell onto our bellies to crawl through a tunnel to the coalface. I could not have been more grateful that this was not my life.

I used to call into police stations to see if anything was going on and learned that thieves had stolen some concrete gnomes from a suburban front garden – all 30 of them. Off I went to the house and the owner of the gnomes spoke about them as if they were her children and told me all about them one by one. She was heartbroken that they had been 'kidnapped.' These little dwarfs, there to guard underground treasures as gnomes do, were as real to her as if they could dance and sing. The whole office was hooting at this daft tale, which filled almost half a page with pictures of the distraught woman and a few gnomes she still had left, and they put it on the street billboards as a bit of a laugh – 'Major Gnome Heist, Big Police Hunt.'

One assignment the paper gave me was to investigate pubs that charged customers more than the brewery-decreed price for beer. I looked at John Cross, the news editor – a perfect name for him – and asked if he was seriously telling me to go and drink beer on expenses. Yes, he was seriously saying that. And how long should this investigation last? As long as necessary. Well, what can one say? It was a good story because over-charging was rampant, but working on it was far-reaching for me personally. It changed my life.

The Earlsden Arms pub was where I ended up one night on this booze-up on expenses. The barmaid, Victoria, was a redhead eight years my senior with a wonderfully soulful face I could not take my eyes off. We immediately hit it off. I drank myself to a standstill and in the morning woke up in an unknown bed. And there she was, beside me. She had poured me into her car and taken me to her house, where I lived for the next 12 months. She wasn't the kind of woman who picked up strange men, but she said I seemed perfectly harmless. Phyllis and I went separate ways.

I learned a great deal from Victoria, who came from a moneyed background (her father owned a chain of off-licences in and around Coventry called Bablake Wines and lived in a grand house with a tennis court). She was sophisticated, I was sandpaper rough. Moving among her circle of friends introduced me to a new world. I got on with her father, a self-made man, and he invited me to grand events in Coventry's higher social circles. I changed in that year more than any year before or since.

Victoria was a talented artist. She had poise and gravitas

and while not classically beautiful she was, to my mind, stunning, with a beautiful voice and lovely red hair. On the one occasion my parents met her my dad whispered: 'Bit upmarket for you.' My mother took against her, of course, condemning her as 'a woman of the world,' whatever that was supposed to mean.

Victoria and I tacitly understood that our relationship was not meant to last. I was young and restless, and after a year I announced that I was leaving to work abroad. There were no scenes, no arguments, only mutual tears. It was one of the hardest decisions I've ever had to make because we had shared a special time, and I look back on it as a pivotal period in my life. Decades later we met up at a pub in Cornwall, where she lived alone in a National Trust cottage overlooking the sea. She slept at night in the garden in a gypsy caravan she had personally restored and decorated with an artist's eye. 'You're not the person I knew,' she told me. 'You're not hungry. It doesn't suit you.'

CHAPTER FOUR

My new hometown rose out of an infinity of scrubland occupied by absolutely nobody, and my first reaction as the plane circled to land was: what's it doing down there in the middle of nowhere? Spider-webs of streets were lined by unimpressive look-alike houses, most with red or green painted tin roofs that sparked in the sunlight. The place was shambolic, as if thrown together in a frantic rush – which it had been, by tens of thousands of roughneck miners a century earlier. I was about to land in the old diamond-mining town of Kimberley, South Africa.

I dragged my big suitcase out of the airport to find a taxi, feeling this was as alien as any place could be. I knew next to nothing about it, knew nobody, had no idea what to expect and didn't speak a word of the main local language. It was thrilling. The taxi took me to an apartment-hotel in the centre of town that was to be my home, called

The Poplars. Despite its name it was surrounded by giant palm trees. Inside, it was comfortable and adequate, in a dog-eared way. Black maids wearing frilly pinafores darted about; black gardeners cut and mowed; black men with ladders and toolboxes kept the place intact; the hotel guests, all white, stuck to themselves as if harbouring secrets.

When I opened my suitcase I encountered a small teddy bear, smelling of Victoria's favourite perfume and a lovely note from her to go with it. I had left Coventry only a few days earlier, but it felt far away already. I felt ragingly homesick. It was a Friday. Three days later I was to start work as a sub-editor on the local English-language newspaper, a daily.

That weekend I spent hours walking the streets to take in the mood, the feeling, the pulse. Everything felt strangely subdued. Perhaps 'suppressed' would be the better word. On Saturday night I drank beer called Rogue Elephant in a bar called The Half Way House, which had tall stools at an immensely high bar from which miners used to drink on horseback. It had swing-doors like a Western saloon and became honky-tonk raucous as the night wore on, the air thick with smoke and expletives.

Here, at least, the throb of life was strong. Those who spoke in English did so with a thick accent I didn't much like but which I nevertheless absorbed over the next two years, and even picked up the tic of inserting 'man' into every fifth sentence. I was about to start work on a newspaper called the *Diamond Fields Advertiser*, whose modest circulation spread far and wide in little communities dotted in and around the Kalahari Desert. It was once controlled by Cecil Rhodes, founder of Rhodesia (Zimbabwe).

The town fanned out from the Big Hole, the biggest man-dug hole in the world, the best part of half a mile deep before rubble and water partially filled it. The clamour for diamonds was why Kimberley existed, and once I got to know the place I couldn't see much point to it now most of the diamonds were gone. Its life-blood, its energy, had left with them, and it emitted the burned-out lethargy of somewhere that had over-heated with dreams and dramas. There were still a few small out-of-town mines, but they were in their death throes. I stood on the edge of the Big Hole – it was about a mile around the perimeter – and imagined thousands of miners down there, hacking at it with picks and shovels in 40 years of frenzy until it was abandoned in 1914.

Kimberley made Rhodes rich and was therefore centre-stage in the South Africa story. It still had the rough airs of a mining town, its people inclined to be distant and suspicious. There were picaresque characters but many were menacing, as if the desert had produced them and baked them hard. These types were easily roused, and any criticism of their country or any questioning of apartheid would have them picking a fight and telling you to fuck off back to England. They were throwbacks to when this was a brawlers' town.

I learned to tiptoe around it, fearful of stepping on its many sensibilities. Everybody had raw nerves. There were a lot of Zulus and Tswana, as well as some Xhosa, all of whom wore their resentment of white domination in eloquent silence. Afrikaners, a lost and lonely tribe, were angry with a world that despised them. They hated the English, as did English-speaking South African whites. Nobody laid out the welcome mat for me.

I got the job at the DFA, as everybody called the paper, by applying to the Argus newspaper group through its London office. I thought I would be going to Cape Town or Johannesburg, but Kimberly is where they sent me, a town still without its first traffic lights. I worked as a sub-editor because I didn't speak Afrikaans, and Afrikaners made up most of the local white population. Sub-editing was not my forte: I would have preferred to be out and about doing stories.

The chief sub-editor was a steady fellow called Brian, who took his day off on Fridays when a grand silver-haired Irishman known as Mr Mac took charge. He always handed the paper to me to design and I went mad with it – whopping great headlines, big pictures and snazzy designs that the printers used to moan about. The chief printer was pure aggression: sun-shrivelled, stick thin, nasty, and anti-English to his bones. He didn't like Afrikaners either, and none worked in the print works. The mutual disdain between Afrikaners and English-speaking whites bubbled under the surface in this isolated little town with its hot-tempered history. Different black tribes didn't get on either. It fizzed with tension.

The biggest local crime was IDB – illicit diamond buying. One of the paper's printers, Baz, a corpulent trencherman who drank and ate with abandon, was into it big-time and often carried a fortune in uncut diamonds inside his socks. He bought the stones from black miners who hid them by swallowing them, risking a terrible gut-ripping death or half a lifetime in jail. When drunk at the Half Way House he would sometimes display them. 'This here,' he said, showing a palm-full, 'would buy you a big house in London and a Rolls Royce to park in the drive.' He didn't need to work, but chose to. The police never bothered him, so I suppose he bribed them.

An important balm to life in Kimberley was the Green Room, an after-hours illegal drinking joint – a shebeen – where the reporters and sub-editors went after putting the paper to bed at 11pm. We had to knock at the door (coloured green) and present ourselves at the peephole. There we would stay for much of the night, enjoying the slow smoky mood, soft sofas and gentle buzz of illegal privilege.

A new trainee reporter called Patricia joined the paper and arrested my attention with her shock of thick red hair, within which was a startlingly white Scottish face. She was just shy of 18 and I was 22, and pretty soon we were a couple. She was born in Edinburgh but had lived in South Africa since she was five, when her mother and plumber father emigrated. She spoke Afrikaans, and I learned quite a bit of it from her.

Patricia had been raised in a company-owned town deep in the bush outside Kimberley where her dad worked, called Ulco (Union Lime Company). It had a company bar, company shop and a company school. Everybody lived in company houses, visited the company doctor and on Sundays attended the company church if they were so inclined. Ulco contained around 200 people locked together in this outpost 50 miles from anywhere.

The journey from Kimberley to Ulco was on a dirt road corrugated like a washboard from the brutal summer heat. On the way there was a scruffy little town called Hotezel, because that's what it was – hot as hell. It was mostly populated by leather-skinned Afrikaner farmers with thick beards and piss-off attitudes towards strangers. I spent one Christmas in Ulco, when everybody sent cards with robins and snow scenes on them when it was 44 degrees outside.

The Afrikaners in Kimberley were a tight-knitted group, light on humour, heavy on religion, formal in company. I can still say in Afrikaans, 'Can I have the honour to dance with you?' because that was how one had to approach an Afrikaans girl at any social event. The ugliest monument to any race of people is assuredly the Voortrekker Monument in Pretoria, a great slab of intricately carved dark stone that somehow captures the gravid essence of those it commemorates. Every Afrikaner I ever met would eventually get around to talking about the Great Trek that this monument recalls, when thousands of Afrikaners left British-controlled Cape Colony in the 1830s to establish a homeland in the middle of southern Africa – a freedom march with glorious mythology that is frequently recalled, and a shameful reality that never is.

Those Boers – meaning farmers – murdered Africans at will, used black children as slaves, stole land and displaced vast numbers of people with the power of their muzzle-loading rifles. What these Voortrekkers – it means 'pathfinders' – endured was phenomenal: the weather, the terrain, attacks by African tribes, scarce water, and malarial mosquitoes that killed many of them as well as the oxen that dragged their carts. Not that they were alone in their slaughter of innocents: Cecil Rhodes came along later and did a much bigger job of it with a machine gun called the Gatling.

I boned up on the Boer Wars and visited some of the battlegrounds. After 14-odd hours on a painfully slow old train – any incline slowed it to walking speed, and it stopped at every speck of a farming settlement for no fathomable reason – I reached Mafeking, which produced one of the great sieges of British colonial history under the leadership of Colonel Baden-Powell, later the founder of the Scouts. For seven months a British military contingent, woefully outnumbered and outgunned by the surrounding Boers, lived on starvation rations. The officers' bunker was still there, albeit mostly caved in, and I could still make out the places where soldiers had dug trenches, now mostly filled in by the wind.

A thousand British troops fought in this burned and useless scrubland in northern Cape Province, not for buildings or territories or critical strategic gain, but simply to stay alive. That's what lent it such power as I wandered around alone. The siege was fed into the popular imagination back home by four British journalists who were there throughout, including one from *The Times*. Their stories were carried to the nearest telegraph office 50 miles away by African runners who slipped through enemy lines at night. What glorious tales those four foreign correspondents harboured in their notebooks.

The relief of Mafeking produced such an explosion of celebration in London its very name was used to describe any kind of friendly racket or raucous celebration. Victorian mothers would yell at their children to 'stop mafeking around.' One delightful little anecdote has always stuck with me: when, at the end of the siege, the leader of the Boer forces was captured, Baden-Powell invited him to dinner.

When I was on the *Thurrock Gazette* I met Lady Baden-Powell, the old soldier's elderly widow – she bore the glorious Christian name of Olave St Clair – who was passing through on some official engagement to do with the Scouts. She was many years younger than her late husband and seemed to me as if she had stepped out of history. I remember very precisely something she said to me: 'Young man, live your life as if you are going to die tomorrow and plan your life as if you are going to live for ever.' I suppose she told that to all the young men she met on her Scouting rounds.

On several occasions I visited a Boer War battlefield near Kimberley called Magersfontein, where the Boers massacred the Scottish Highland Brigade and the Black Watch in 1899. It was a ghostly place in the quiet desert breezes, the trenches of warfare still just about distinguishable. The wounded died on the ground in their kilts, legs blistering in the December summer sun. A bugler boy was shot out of the saddle two or three times but each time climbed back up and continued sounding the attack until he was shot dead.

The Boers honoured him by burying him alongside their own, along with a plaque written in English to commemorate his bravery, describing him merely as an unknown Scottish bugler.

Many years later, on a visit with Valerie to show her where I used to live, I discovered that his name had been identified and there it was, right there, albeit nearly a century late, on a little plaque all by itself. He was Drummer William Milne of the Seaforth Highlanders. I felt absurdly happy and moved about that. And I think it would be fair to mention that during this visit I discovered that Kimberley had evolved beyond recognition into a decent little town, and that the Half Way House had become very posh and no longer had swing doors nor a high bar for miners on horseback. The Big Hole had been turned into a tourist site, the town now boasted traffic lights, and the Poplars apartment-hotel was gone. Most amazingly of all, a statue of Cecil Rhodes still stood in the heart of the town, mounted on a giant bronze horse.

I spent all my holiday time travelling. On one trip I took a train that was to have transported me almost to Lesotho, that landlocked little country in the middle of South Africa, but I ended up stranded far from my destination at a tiny railway station deep in the desert with no passenger train due for days. I was informed of this alarming news by the driver of the train that had just dropped me there before heading off for essential repairs. I stood alone on the platform in this tumbleweed-strewn no-man's-land beneath a big empty sky and had no plans whatsoever, save to wait for something to happen. There was a tap that produced water so I wouldn't die of thirst.

I thought I might be sleeping on the floor that night, hungry, but after some hours I saw a cloud of dust moving my way in the far distance along a track that passed by the station. An astonishingly old pickup truck approached, rattling and groaning. I flagged it down and an Afrikaner farmer with broken English told me a goods train was likely to pass through later and I could hitch a ride.

And so it transpired. It was hauling a huge line of wagons and as it approached I waved at the driver in the hope that he would stop, which he did in a cacophony of clanking and banging. It was heading to my original destination on the outskirts of Lesotho. I passed the journey with the Afrikaner driver on the footplate as we clattered through the desert, mostly in silence because his English was poor. When we arrived I found somewhere to eat and sleep, and next day took a bus to Maseru, the Lesotho capital.

I befriended a student who invited me to a party that night at his university, which was a long way out of town. I accepted, which was a bad call. It was soon obvious that none of the other students liked the presence of this white man and they became hostile. My friend told me to follow him quickly to his room. A crowd began banging on the locked door, so we climbed out the window and ran into the bush. My friend took me to a place to hide, wished me luck, and left. I stayed there until dawn when a bus came down the road leading back to Maseru, as I had been assured it would.

I ran from my hiding place, flagged it down and escaped. The bus was testimony to mechanical creativity: it was a wreck on wheels, with a windscreen so cracked and splintered it was a wonder the driver could see anything at all.

South Africa held me in thrall with its big spaces, open skies and raw, hard beauty. I loved the Kalahari Desert because it bore the thrill of being utterly different from anything I had known, with its springboks, huge ant-hills, baked-red soil, giant cactuses, great big kudu that would sometimes leap into the road in front of you, and the occasional little bushmen who popped up out of nowhere, nervous as birds.

At weekends Patricia and I would take off to a natural lake about 20 miles outside Kimberley called Scotsman's Pool and leap into its warm waters from a great height from the surrounding cliffs without ever managing to touch the bottom. Being abroad felt thrilling: being somewhere so powerfully and definitively abroad was exotic. My becoming a foreign correspondent was no longer just a fiercely-held dream: my experiences in South Africa had turned it into a compulsion, which is why I had to return to London to pursue it.

There had been times when I thought vaguely about staying, not in roughshod little Kimberley but in Johannesburg or Cape Town where the journalism was bigger and language no barrier. But there were competing voices, both professional and personal. Apartheid was not right, not moral, and I had reached the point where I couldn't bear it.

The first and only black African I ever asked to stop calling me *Baas*, and to use my name, was called Betty, a maid at Poplars Hotel. She told me she would be reported to the police if she called me by name, because it would suggest an improper intimacy. We were always on friendly terms and when we said goodbye every bit of me wanted to give her a hug, but all hell would have broken loose had we been seen.

Patricia and I sailed to Southampton on the *Union Castle* from Cape Town and had a year together before our rival cultural experiences proved too much. She belonged where she had been raised, missed her parents, and needed to go home. We stayed erratically in touch, however, and the last I heard from her, fully 30 years after we parted, was that she and her husband had been mugged in their Johannesburg home. Patricia was tied up but not harmed. Her husband was severely pistol-whipped about the head and was never able to work again. All the intruders stole was a television and the family car, which was abandoned and torched a few miles away. She never wrote again.

CHAPTER FIVE

Back in England, my South African accent refused to relent. I could hear it in my head but not remove it from my tongue. It's not the sweetest sound: not a singing Welsh or a lilting Irish, not a slightly comical Australian nor an American Deep South song, but this hammer-blow that has no welcoming place beyond its own geography. I still wanted to say *bioscope* for cinema and *braaivleis* for a barbecue, and around Patricia when we were together in England it was going nowhere because she talked like Nelson Mandela. It took two years before people stopped asking where I was from.

I spoke that way because I had taken the advice of a man who said I should go abroad to get more journalistic and life experience, and then he might think of employing me. As soon as I reached England I contacted him, and he invited me for an interview. He remembered the advice he had given me in response to a plaintive letter of mine, and was impressed that I had taken it. He was managing editor of *The Times*, and he didn't hire journalists younger than 24. I was two weeks shy of that. Six days after my 24th birthday I went on the payroll.

I was put on a three-month trial as a parliamentary gallery reporter, which I survived, and my job was what a *Guardian* journalist contemptuously described to me as a *shorthand prol*. The woman was right. I didn't write stories: I quoted words, without analysis, without any writing whatsoever. Whenever an MP or minister said something interesting I wrote it down and it appeared in long grey columns as a sort of mini-Hansard record of parliamentary procedures. It wasn't journalism, it was shorthand-writing, but it was a foot in the door of a great newspaper – albeit the back door.

One perk of the job was being free to do shifts for Hansard, the official record of the proceedings of Parliament, when *The Times* had done with me for the night, which was a vital boost to my income, having acquired a mortgage well beyond my means. The hours were long and wearying when Hansard was added to the mix, and the late-night commute home always a trial. On more than one occasion I fell asleep on the late train home, ended up at the end of the line 15 miles beyond my station, crossed over, did exactly the same in reverse and woke up back in London. The worst part of the job was covering the House of Lords, that chamber of snores and bores where everybody wibbles on and on in subdued voices as if gathered round a deathbed. The debates were sometimes so soporific I would slide into a corner of the invariably empty Press benches and catch up on sleep, confident that nobody would say a word worth reporting.

Once a week I went to the print-works to put the parliamentary page to bed. It was a place of noise and hot lead, and the smell of printers' ink to this day has me swooning in nostalgia. The lead typefaces were assembled in a metal frame called the *chase*, and I would have a friendly banter with the printer as he sorted out the articles and headlines.

'Where did I put that bloody headline?' one printer asked me. I saw it, picked it up, and handed it to him. Journalists did NOT touch printers' lead. It was cosmic law. More important than that, it was a rule laid down by the National Graphical Association, the print union, whose militant heart was itself made of solid lead.

'Father of the chapel!' he boomed above the racket of linotype machines. 'A journalist touched the lead!' Every linotype machine went silent. A hush descended and all eyes turned to me. The headline was still in my hand, like a smoking gun. The first edition of the paper was lost while the matter was discussed in huddles among the father of the chapel and fellow union bosses. They kept this going long enough to lose the first edition, which meant there would be no copies of *The Times* the following day in Scotland or Wales. Having wrought enough damage to slake their ire, they allowed printing to resume. I thought I would be in big trouble with the paper's management, but nobody said anything to me about it. The unions stopped the paper so often in those anarchic days of trade union militancy it was a surprise when they didn't. My own union, the National

Union of Journalists, fell under hard-left influence and I resigned from it, never to rejoin.

There were twelve of us Press Gallery reporters, all aware that our jobs were more stenography than journalism. I begged to be sent to the newsroom but was told my shorthand was too valuable where I was. The very skill that had carried me so far was now paradoxically holding me back. I was proud to say I worked at *The Times* but didn't feel like a journalist any more. I did get to do some stints in the newsroom during the long parliamentary recesses but mostly I sat around getting in the way, an unwanted and untried extra hand without a desk to sit at.

Valerie supported me when I decided to resign from *The Times*, because after four years of parliamentary gallery reporting I couldn't stand it any more. One morning I walked out of our flat with my resignation letter in my pocket, with no future plans save for some half-cocked idea to go to Africa and set myself up as a freelance Africa correspondent. I didn't think of the consequences of quitting: it was one of those instinctive, resolute decisions possessed of the young, and which the fates are often inclined to reward. And they did. Fast.

I was barely out the door when Valerie called me back, saying I had a call from somebody describing himself as Labour Editor of *The Times* – a fellow called Paul Routledge. He said he had a job that might interest me. A minute later and it would have been too late to stop me boarding a train to London and handing in my resignation. Of such moments are miracles made. What if I had left a minute earlier? Or

Routledge had called a minute later? Or Valerie hadn't been home? Or she had been on the phone when he rang?

I met him at the Cheshire Cheese in Fleet Street that lunchtime. I entered the upstairs bar, a pleasingly rough-and-ready place with sawdust on the floor, and looked around for an elegant, imposing figure whose by-lined stories I had often read with awe. It took a while to identify him because he was short, dumpy, spoke with a Yorkshire accent, was well into his third pint – three more would follow – and had a laugh that made the glasses rattle. He gave the immediate impression of being quite brilliant.

We shook hands.

'Can you hold your drink?' he asked.

'Yes.'

'You're hired. What'll it be?'

It was the best job interview I had ever done and I only said one word – but the right one. When I left the pub I took out my resignation letter, tore it up and dropped it into a bin. And then I walked up and down Fleet Street telling myself I was at last going to be a proper journalist on the grandest paper of them all. I called Val and she squealed with delight. She wouldn't have to live in Windhoek after all.

I became Labour Reporter, which meant covering trade union affairs, the third man in a three-man team, and in due course was promoted to second man. It was touch-and-go at the beginning though. My first assignment was to cover a strike at British Leyland in Oxford, when I called a union leader a communist who wasn't one, and if that wasn't bad enough I didn't have a clue what the story was about and made a hash of it.

I followed a *Financial Times* journalist into a pub, hoping but failing to pick his brains, and watched him confidently write out his story in a notebook over a pint of beer before going outside to a phone box to dictate it. I, on the other hand, was paralysed. I had a notebook full of stuff that meant nothing to me. I simply couldn't fathom what the story was about. British Leyland management had given a press conference and union leaders had talked to the press on the street, but none of it added up. I was unable to write a single paragraph and ended up sitting in a launderette because it was now dark and it had lights on. I stared at my notebook in terror.

In the end I had to file something, anything, and after doing so I disappeared so I couldn't be contacted by the news desk. My story was a shambling mess despite being knocked around by the sub-editors to make some sense out of it. I knew then that I was way out of my depth on this big bloody newspaper with its big bloody stories and big clever reporters. I was by my own estimation the most working-class reporter on the paper, swimming among a self-assured clerisy of grammar schoolers and university graduates, feeling fearful of exposure and humiliation.

'Unimpressed with that,' Routledge said when I turned up at the office next day. The non-communist I had libelled was paid modest damages to stop it going to court, and I was a marked man. It took quite a while to climb out of that hole, but gradually it was forgotten, except by me. It knocked every bit of self-belief out of me for a long time, and I envied people who did jobs that came easily to them. I pressed on nervously, terrified of another blunder, which would probably have been fatal. Little by little, I settled in.

The labour beat was wild living. It was drinking at lunchtime with bibulous union officials and drinking at night with them again, which is why Routledge had asked me if I could hold my booze. No union officials ever bought a round because they knew you were on expenses. It meant staying out too late to go home and crashing out in hotels and it meant learning how to dictate copy half drunk, often from an illegal after-hours underground drinking den in Fleet Street called the Golf Club, which had absolutely nothing to do with golf. It was there, essentially, for journalists, and it had a huge bank of payphones for our benefit. The police kindly left it alone.

Many a time I filed from that dark space, and the copy-takers were always marvellous. 'Chris old chap, you already said that four paragraphs ago.' Or, 'You're coming up for 700 words now. Shouldn't you be wrapping it up?' Sometimes they would say something like 'nice story mate' and send you off feeling chuffed.

I would often be out late enough to head to the printworks to pick up a copy of the paper to see where my story figured in it. The roar of fork-lift trucks, the revving of delivery lorries, the shouting men, the smell of ink, the air of urgency, the frantic clatter of the presses – it was all so bloody exciting. I would look into the bowels of the building and see hundreds of thousands of newspapers in there, an unbelievable mass, all heading to every corner of the country with my words in them.

I did this job for more than four years, and apart from a chaotic start I loved it. The labour beat was one of the most important of that era because industrial action was a national disease, a time when questions were asked like, 'Who runs Britain?' I mingled with union leaders as famous as Cabinet ministers, and they all seemed like my dad when you got behind the mask.

It was a time when even the firemen went on strike. The car workers were always on strike; the railways were on strike; it was one round of industrial warfare after another, and the three of us were never out of the paper. I spent untold hours door-stepping 10 Downing Street waiting for union leaders to emerge from crisis talks. To impress their memberships they would issue belligerent statements, which we would all file, and then we hacks went off to meet them in the pub where they got pissed on our expense account money and whispered about where the next strike would be. Sometimes it would be at the newspapers themselves. On occasions they would stop a paper because they didn't like something in it, which raised a furious debate about freedom of the press.

It was during my time on the labour beat that *The Times* closed for a full year because of a fight with the print unions over the introduction of computerised printing technology. The unions were destroying the industry with endless strikes. Printers signed on as Mickey Mouse and Roy Rogers and got paid nevertheless because they were unsackable. They earned more than High Court judges. Some had homes in Spain or France and rarely, if ever, reported for work, but still got paid. The battle over new technology was going to be decisive for the survival of newspapers, and it turned ugly.

It fell to me to report on the impending closure of the paper. I dealt with everybody from the top floor to the shop floor, so I knew as much about the dispute as anybody. The time came when I was to write the definitive op-ed piece shortly before the paper closed indefinitely, headlined 'Why *The Times* Is Closing,' or words similar, and it was rejected by the editor, William Rees-Mogg, for slanting too far towards the union viewpoint. Unless I changed it, he wouldn't publish it.

I told him he was censoring me and charged out of his office, flinging back the door as I did so, and stopped dead when I heard it tear off its hinges. Oh Christ, I thought, that's that then. A day or two later the paper closed, all the journalists had a year off on full pay until it reopened, and nobody ever said a word to me about my appalling conduct. I guess people had bigger things to worry about. The article appeared in full with not a word altered. When the paper reopened I immediately applied for another job, and – thanks entirely to Valerie – I got it.

CHAPTER SIX

A man to conjure with: Louis Heren, a blunt-edged East Ender who worked his way up from messenger boy on *The Times* to the paper's most senior foreign correspondent, ending up as Washington bureau chief. He came within a whisker of being appointed editor but Rupert Murdoch, who had just bought the paper, said he was too old. After perhaps 30 years working around the world, Louis returned to be the senior home news editor and later became deputy editor. He never fully lost traces of his Cockney accent and walked with a swaying gait as if pushing a barrow down Spitalfields. He once roasted me for wearing a donkey jacket to work. 'You're a journalist on *The Times*, not a docker,' he barked.

He told exotic stories about his adventures and wrote a book called *Growing Up On The Times*. I wanted a life like his and told him so. Some of the haughtier journalists were appalled when he was appointed deputy editor, considering him to be not quite the right cut: this stocky little man with crumpled clothes and fuck-you airs and no university degree.

One day he discreetly invited Valerie to a smart restaurant for lunch and told her he had plans for me, but wanted to check with her first because he wasn't in the business of breaking marriages. 'If you don't want to go along with this, nobody will ever know except you and me. If you say no, then this conversation never took place. Chris will never know.' That was Val's account of the conversation.

To which she responded: 'But I would know and I couldn't live with that. The answer is yes. I'll go.'

And so Louis gave me the job I had applied for. I was to be Ireland Correspondent, based in Belfast at a time when Ulster was ablaze and not best suited to raising three children. The posting was a recognised stepping stone to becoming a foreign correspondent if you didn't screw up.

Within a month we were there. Initially we lived in a remote bungalow overlooking Strangford Lough in Newtownards, County Down, a house so cold we often wore coats indoors. The only heating seeped out of open fires burning coal or turf; candles would have been as effective. The wind sliced off the lake with nothing to impede it, muscling its way into the house through ill-fitting windows that rattled constantly like background music. We slept under heavy blankets most of the year. Mornings could be torture. Statistically it rained every second day so we shared the house with damp, mould and rust. We had inherited this dreadful property from my predecessor and immediately started looking for somewhere else.

Meanwhile, we all retreated quite frequently to the cheery hearths of a pub in the charming small town of Portaferry 20 miles away, where the priests gathered on Sundays to drink halves of Guinness between services and the customers were nearly all Catholics in a largely Protestant area. There was never any trouble, though. Sometimes I would sit in the dim warmth of a stone-built pub in a nearby Protestant village called Greyabbey, frequented by off-duty policemen who would tell everybody when the road was safe from drink-driving checks.

We enrolled our daughter Melanie in the local primary school and on her first day she was told to stand on a desk in the front row for failing to pay attention. The backs of her legs were struck with a ruler and when Valerie went to pick her up at the end of the school day the child was hysterical. Her only crime was that she hadn't understood the teacher's accent. I went to the school next day and raged at the whole bloody lot of them. Bashing children in schools in Northern Ireland was what they did then. Wasn't there enough violence to go around already?

I also had trouble when we went to enrol Maria in the same school when she reached the age of five. Mr McGibney, the headmaster, was clearly bothered by her name and indirectly inquired if she was Catholic because, he indicated, he didn't want any of that sort in his school. I told him it was none of his business, he said it was, and we remained at a stalemate until I told him I was going to make him famous. 'It's a good story,' I said with grand pomposity. 'I can see the headline: *School Bans Child Because Her Name Is Maria*. She got in. She was Church of England, but I never told McGibney.

Our bungalow's one redeeming feature was its panoramic view of Strangford Lough, apart, that is, from our delightful neighbour, Peter, who was also the landlord and punctuated his conversation with 'dead-on.' He quietly expressed concern when a British Army officer – Colonel Pipe, I recall – I had invited for dinner turned up in a growling military vehicle with two squaddies carrying rifles, who stationed themselves like sentries outside the front door for the entire evening. 'Draws attention to us, you see,' he pointed out, and I promised to ask my guests to be more discreet in future. 'Dead-on,' he said.

He had one further occasion to raise objections. I had been to a wet lunch in army headquarters in Lisburn with a bunch of other journalists and a senior officer who had become something of a friend offered to give me a lift home. Lovely, thanks, very kind, I said, and he walked me off to find my ride. Next up, I was sitting in a helicopter and off we went to my house, dropping gently into a field behind it. My car was delivered to the house next day by soldiers. Peter wasn't 'dead-on' about that, either.

Right beneath the house was the yacht club. I bought a small boat with an underpowered outboard engine, and one fine day – there were one of two every year – I went out in it with several boozy journalists visiting from London. The one who was most incapacitated by indulgence was an elegant fellow from the *Morning Star* (the communists took a keen interest in Ulster). He was due to give a speech that evening to people of a similar persuasion, and was dressed in a suit and tie.

Which was a pity, because he fell overboard.

Strangford Lough has a devilishly strong current. It's tidal. It moves towards Portaferry on its way out to the ocean, where it is funnelled into a narrow channel and charges through with phenomenal power before doing exactly the same on the way back. One way or another it's always thrashing about. Getting to the poor floundering communist – who was shouting that he couldn't swim – was difficult, but I managed it despite the feebleness of my outboard engine. He stumbled ashore looking cold and dejected and very sober. That little escapade got into *Private Eye*. I wish I knew which sneak did that.

After getting into trouble in that boat one more time, with Melanie aboard this time – another boat had to rescue us as we were being propelled by the tide towards Portaferry and oblivion – I got rid of it.

There had to be a frivolous side in times like those. Being Ireland Correspondent was a seven-day-a-week job, always waiting for the next bad thing to happen. It meant being stopped now and then by masked men with guns; it meant not knowing if the nice man you were talking to at the Sinn Fein office on the Falls Road was somebody nasty in the IRA. It meant watching a chatty IRA-linked man bouncing his little boy on his knee while telling you why it was necessary to murder British soldiers and plant bombs in shopping centres. It was hearing Protestant people talk about Catholics (Taigs, they called them) as though they were from another planet. It meant watching eight-year-olds with cans of spray-paint daubing 'REMEMBER 1690' on the sides of buildings. It meant meeting an IRA man in the middle of a busy traffic intersection because long-range army listening devices couldn't penetrate the traffic noise.

It meant having my house bombed, with the family inside.

Not that our house was a target, but sometimes a badly-built bomb went off in the wrong direction. We lived right on the shoreline in Bangor, in County Down (we had moved from our refrigerated bungalow in Newtownards), and the Co-op supermarket, the intended target, was on the other side of the bay. Our house and the houses next door took the brunt of the bomb, leaving the Co-op with little more than broken windows. It was a Saturday lunchtime. Our house was fully 400 yards away from the bomb: much closer and it would have been obliterated. I was in Belfast in the office catching up with chores on my one theoretical day off a week, when I heard on the inimitable Downtown Radio – always the first with news of terrorist attacks – that Bangor had been hit by a huge bomb. Oh dear God, my family.

Before I had a chance to leave the office I got hit by a bomb of my own. It was targeted at the Presbyterian Church across from my office on the fifth floor of the Europa Hotel (the most bombed hotel in the world at the time, boasting 36 bomb attacks, and still it stands). I was lifted very slowly off my feet, or so it seemed, and slammed forcefully against the wall. Energy waves are amazing. I was dizzy but unhurt. The windows didn't smash, so I can only imagine they contained some sort of reinforced glass.

There was no reply when I rang home. I knew from Downtown Radio that the bomb had gone off near our house and no 30-minute journey was ever as long as that one. When the police and army stopped me on the outskirts of the town my heart nearly burst out of me because clouds of black smoke were rising high into the sky and sirens were sounding everywhere. I showed my press pass and was allowed to continue on foot. The house was a mile away.

I ran through the streets and then saw it, smashed up at the front, right there on Queen's Parade. I stood there for a moment and said, quite clearly to myself, that what I discovered in the next five minutes would shape the rest of my life. I walked to the house, afraid to run, afraid of what I would discover. And there, at the back of it, unharmed, I found Valerie and our three children, one of them, Matthew, just a toddler sucking his dummy without a care in the world.

What happened in the following minutes and hours is a total blank to me. For reasons I don't understand it has been wiped from my memory. I cannot remember anything of detail about what was said between us. I cannot fully picture the damage to the house, except knowing that it was uninhabitable. I cannot remember taking my family away from it, I don't remember comforting anybody, I have no recollection of where we all spent that night – it has all been lost to me. All I know is that the family moved swiftly to England and stayed there until my days in Belfast were done, which was only a matter of weeks away because I had been assigned elsewhere. I moved into my office in the Europa Hotel after that, just me and the job and a lot of take-aways and room service.

I asked Melanie to describe the events of that day, because she was old enough to remember.

'It was a weekend morning. Matthew was napping in his cot in the bedroom at the back of the house and never woke up. Maria and I were playing in my room. Mum was in her bedroom. There was a boom and we ran to Mum, scared. The force of the explosion had thrown her across the room. Dylan (our dog) was under the bed trembling. People were pouring onto the streets. I went outside in my pink fluffy slippers. I heard people talking about a bomb at the Co-op supermarket, the one I went to all the time with Maria. All the windows of the front of our house were blown in.'

Towards the end of this assignment I felt drained. I wasn't aware of how deeply the story was getting to me until a simple incident triggered a very un-simple response. It happened – it's almost absurd to say this – when a sparrow smashed into the windscreen of my car and lay dead in the road behind me. Just that. One sparrow set against all the ghastly stuff I had covered stripped me bare. It happened on my way up the beautiful Antrim coast on a day's outing to get away from the hothouse of Belfast one Saturday. I was alone.

I stopped the car with a squeal of tyres as if I had hit a child. There in the road, through the rear-view mirror, I saw the bird. And then a whole flock of sparrows settled on a telephone wire and looked down at it. They just perched there, staring, dozens of them, all totally quiet. Now and then, two or three fluttered down to investigate.

What an absurd trigger this was. You report about a man who was watching television when two gunmen shot him in front of his wife and children; you cover the story of a teenager shot in both knees and forever condemned to limp with sticks because he disobeyed ghetto-law; you write about the five dead, the ten dead, the 40 dead, in a single atrocity; and you never know how much it has been building up inside you until it comes gushing out.

It is one thing to read about an atrocity, another to see it. That really brings it home. I knew there had been historical injustices, that awful wrongs were done over a very long time that we British shamefully ignored or perpetrated, but how does anybody ever reach a point of hatred when it feels right to blow your neighbours to pieces? I tried to comprehend the mind that can set a bomb in the middle of a crowd, but what was always most difficult to understand was the point of it: in a purely cold political and strategic sense, what could all that slaughter possibly achieve that was worth having? Could anything justify 2000-odd violent deaths and thousands injured?

And then you ask this: how does the bomb-planter live with himself when he sees on the nightly news innocent people being carried away in ambulances, maimed or dead? Will he say to himself: I did that and damn you all? Was there a ripple of regret? Or a sense of triumph, a fuck-you-too, that's payback for what you did to us through history? Did he talk to his wife about it as he watched the news? Go to a bar and get drunk? Tell a friend? Make a cup of tea and not think about it? Did he have to keep it to himself because walls have ears? How did he sleep that night? Did it haunt him a year later? How did he *feel* afterwards? How would he feel years later? Did he ever ask himself what difference it made in the end, killing those people? Did he ever ask himself if he was wrong? Would he take it back if he could?

The questions go on and on. How can such a person ever be the same after that? How can normal feelings of pity and empathy ever rise in him again? If he saw somebody in the street in a wheelchair, blind, deaf and crippled, did he wonder if his bomb did that to this man, this woman, this child, who never did a thing to harm him?

I once interviewed a former IRA bomber who had spent many years in jail, and he told me he had been young and misguided and regretted it. But he didn't think about it any more. Could it possibly be that simple to erase what he did?

History haunted everything in Ulster. Wherever you turned it confronted you, hot and festering and foul with bad things that were done yesterday, a month ago, a year ago, 20, 50, 300 and 400 years ago. Almost every day you watched more stinking history being piled on top of it, cursing the future of another generation. A few final questions: what kind of society did the bombers and assassins think would emerge out of their workmanship had they succeeded? Can you bomb close to a million people (the Protestants) into something they don't want and expect them to settle down and live with it? Wouldn't they take up arms and fight back? Of course they bloody would.

Valerie was hired by the Northern Irish Education Department to teach primary-age children in their homes when they were too psychologically disturbed by violence to go to school. This job took her to the hidden front lines of the war where the broken people were, where the psychiatrists and physiotherapists were, where the special teachers were to be found, where doctors and nurses did amazing unsung things, a place where there were people who could not walk or see or hear or had lost their minds because somebody planted a bomb or pulled a trigger and ran away.

Most of the children taught by Valerie had seen a relative murdered or had witnessed the carnage of a bomb attack; in some cases they had seen their own father or older brother gunned down in front of them, right in their own homes, three bullets to the head, brains all over the wall. They were incapable of relating to normal society, and there was one child Valerie used to visit who never spoke at all.

One of her students, aged around 11, had watched a masked man put several bullets into his father's head and chest in the family's own living room. Nobody else was at home and the boy just waited there until somebody came. That's a lifetime sentence of trauma. Nothing and nobody can cure a thing like that. Valerie and I were stopped once by an IRA patrol and a masked man shoved a rifle through the window and demanded to know what the fuck I was doing driving a car with English number plates. 'Are you fucking army?' We denied it. 'Ah,' he then said, relaxing and withdrawing the rifle, 'not to worry. Hello Valerie, how are you? Off you go now.' She could never know whose children she was teaching. Kids on both sides were traumatised and needed the help of people like her.

One day I got a phone call from London telling me the startling news that I had been named by an MP in the House of Commons. This MP had asked the Northern Ireland Secretary if he would investigate the activities of a certain Christopher Thomas of *The Times*, 'who is known to those of us in the trade as the enemy wireless.' That MP was called Enoch Powell, who was then an MP for a Northern Irish constituency. He was referring to a series of leaks I had got about an impending government consultation document, known as a Green Paper, exploring ideas for peace in Northern Ireland, and those ideas smelled to Mr Powell like a plot for the reunification of Ireland. There was a small but powerful cabal within the Northern Ireland Office in favour of this, and Powell felt they were the people leaking stuff to me. He was on the mark there.

The phone rang in my office one morning and a voice said: 'This is Lucidia. Get out.' Lucidia was the code-name for the Irish National Liberation Army to authenticate any communications from it. The reason for its ire was a story on the front page of that day's *Times*, with my name on it, which described the political wing of this organisation as 'illegal.' Unfortunately it was not, and the mistake was not mine. A sub-editor had assumed it was a banned organisation and changed my copy without checking.

In discussions between the paper and INLA's political

wing it was agreed no harm would come to me if I remained in Ulster, but the paper would have to publish a letter by way of a correction. When that letter arrived it was a lengthy political rant, and every word was published in the Letters to the Editor page. Many readers and not a few MPs were appalled to read such propaganda, without knowing the background. It was a tough call for the editor.

The most heart-warming story of my experiences in that heart-breaking place concerned a peripatetic Anglican nun called Sister Anna, a jolly lady who belonged to an order that required her – or enabled her, as she preferred to put it – to turn up in different parts of the world to do good works. She had worked all over the planet and had stories galore about the places she had been. She told me that whenever she sensed she was growing roots she would move some-where else. It was the life she loved. I found her by chance in the slums of Belfast, draped in oilskin waterproofs, astride the moped she moved around on. She joked about never wearing her habit in Ulster – her order stipulated the wearing of habits even though it was Protestant. 'Can you imagine the reaction if I did, sitting on a moped poodling down the Shankill Road?' The thought made her chuckle.

Journalists could move freely between the two big Protestant and Catholic ghettoes in Belfast – the Shankill and its Catholic near-neighbour, the Falls Road – without undue fear because journalists were not targets in the conflict. I thought we were the only people able to do that, but Sister Anna did it every day. I joined her on her rounds. We started off amid the squalor of Catholic households and I watched as she listened to people's troubles, always touching them, holding their hands, listening hard. I had never imagined such poverty existed so close to home: entire families with not enough money for the meter, depression hanging heavy in dark little living rooms, everybody with sunken cheeks and bad teeth.

From there we went to the Shankill, and the Protestant families there lived no better. Almost everybody she spoke to on both sides suffered broken health, and all craved peace. Sister Anna would hold them tight while they cried for it. I watched her hugging a tough-looking old man who could take no more; I saw her comfort a single mother with five children and not a coin to her name. Catholic and Protestant, she prayed with them both, but kept it neutral. Try as I might, I could never coax her to venture an opinion on what was going on in Northern Ireland. She cared about helping victims, not questioning why they existed, which is why nobody doubted her neutrality in a place where neutrality was suspect. To build trust in that nervous and explosive environment was a huge achievement. She sought no recognition and had to be persuaded by me over a long time to let me write about her.

Not long after my day with Sister Anna, I went to Dublin for my occasional trawl of events there. On the way back to Belfast I stopped at a bar in the border town of Dundalk to use its payphone to call London because it was close to deadline and I needed to check for queries on my copy. Not one of the public phones I had tried on the roadsides had worked. The news desk did have a question – could I confirm the spelling of Taoiseach (Irish for president)? So I spelled it out, at considerable volume because the line was bad, and became aware that the bar had gone silent. As I went to leave I was stopped by a man sitting on a bar stool who stuck his leg out in front of me.

'Who are you?'

'A journalist from the London *Times*.'

'I smell army on you.'

I showed him my press pass.

'Anybody can get one of those.'

'My hair's too long to be a soldier.'

'Anyone can grow fucking hair.'

Several men took me outside and kicked me around, cracking some ribs. They let me go after a while and I managed to drive off. A couple of them wanted another go and chased me in their car all the way to the border before turning back at the sight of the British Army checkpoint. I never told the paper about it. With so many tragedies everywhere around me it seemed indulgent to complain. I knew the office would want me to write about it, and I knew I wouldn't be able to, having seen what others had to endure every day in unsung anonymity.

I did once take one of those unsung people out of obscurity, at his own request. His name was Roy Kells, a shopkeeper in Lisnaskea in County Fermanagh, close to the Irish border. He was a part-time soldier and seven nights a week went on patrol with the Ulster Defence Regiment, which made him a target for the IRA. Over the years his shop had been bombed three times and set on fire once. When I met him he had just survived his second assassination attempt. It wasn't customary for survivors to be named in the media, but Mr Kells insisted.

He was dressing the window of his drapery store when a young man walked up to the other side of the glass and fired five bullets at him. The thick glass deflected every bullet and only one touched him, grazing his head and drawing blood. He would have been the 65th IRA victim in County Fermanagh in ten years. Eye-witnesses said the gunman slowly lowered his weapon and stood staring at Mr Kells for several seconds, apparently incredulous that he wasn't dead, before escaping on a getaway motorcycle.

Five years earlier Mr Kells was hanging curtains in a local school when a bullet from a high velocity rifle smashed through the window and went into the wall an inch above his head. He posed for a photograph in front of the bullet-holed glass of his shop for my photographer, although we ensured his face was in silhouette. It was important to him to put that image out there, to show what people had to endure and to announce that he would not succumb. He didn't want to say anything on record, but his wife said it for him. 'We intend to carry on. You can't let them force you out.'

There is a housing estate in Belfast called the Ballymurphy, and it was a Republican hotbed that the army patrolled in squat, slow-moving armoured Saracen vehicles known by the troops as Pigs. I was invited to go in one of these vehicles by a certain Brigadier David Ramsbotham on one of its tours around the estate, an experience that gave a feel for the fever and rage of the place. There were four or five soldiers in the vehicle, and the purpose of the patrol was simply to make a statement that Ballymurphy was not a no-go area. Attacking Pigs was a sport for children as much as adults. The children would throw open cans of baked beans at the little opening that the driver looked through, so the tomato sauce would splash through and make a mess. They mixed up 'paint bombs' in balloons and bottles so the vehicles had to be repainted.

Pigs had a device in them that could trace the route of any bullet that hit them or came close, and when that happened a chase would ensue in which the gunman always got away because he had a whole estate of houses to hide in. It was sick sport. It meant the troops would smash down doors and charge through houses, and all for nothing except to feed the fever and excite the young gangs. 'Armoured cars and tanks and guns, came to take away our sons...' It was the stuff of rebel music.

Whenever word was out that a Pig was on the streets, hordes of young people would pour out of their houses to harass them. Inside the vehicle the bottles and bricks smashing against the armour sounded alarmingly loud. The soldiers had heard reports about the IRA acquiring armour-piercing weapons, and made black jokes about what a mess one of those bullets would make if it smashed around inside the vehicle.

When they threw open the back doors to go for a look around – I couldn't understand the point of taking that risk

– people ran away and stood at a distance yelling taunts. The headline on that piece was: 'Ballymurphy's Bombs Bricks and Bullets.' Some colleagues on the paper said they hated it because it was too romantic a depiction of something ghastly. I saw their point and never ventured anything similar.

On my last day in Belfast I was about to walk out of the office for the last time when the phone rang. It was the news desk in London, wanting me to write a valedictory piece for the next day's paper. I dictated 700 words off the top of my head and when I read the article in the paper the next morning it was like reading it for the first time. It had just poured out of me. In it I talked about my need to leave that place; I talked about the cynical manipulation of the people. I started the article by quoting the Catholic politician Gerry Fitt, who once told me, 'the man who understands Ireland is misinformed.' If I had sat down to write that article and given it some thought I wouldn't have had the courage to make it so personal. At the bottom of it – 'A Farewell To Arms,' it was headlined – the sub-editors attached a short sentence: '*Christopher Thomas will be reporting next from New York.*'

CHAPTER SEVEN

Manhattan shimmered into view as we crossed the Brooklyn Bridge, which was like driving through a harp. Valerie laughed at the magnificent audacity of it, a hundred movies old already, full of police sirens and yellow cabs and Marilyn Monroe's legs, Central Park, the Italian quarter, Latin quarter, Harlem, The Village, 5th Avenue, Brooklyn, gangsters and guns, all bundled into a headful of images.

We pulled up to the apartment-hotel that would be home for a month, right in the middle of all the action on 42nd Street with flashing neon signs offering 'Topless Girls! Girls! Girls!' There were bars dark with secrets, and parading up and down the street lots of drug-racked prostitutes offered a cheery 'hi mister!' to any likely john. There were lots of beggars wearing exaggerated rags and holed shoes, a uniform for pavement-work before they changed and caught the bus home.

Something about the way people moved, spoke and related to each other made me feel rather meek and English. Ordinary conversation could sound like a fight. Please and thank-you were effete delicacies that didn't figure in this battering ram of noise. Being assertive and emphatic and very loud were *de rigueur*. Everything commanded an exclamation mark. Everybody was eccentric – well, *different* – in their way of walking, talking, arguing and cussing, and especially in the effusive way they wished each other a nice day with smiles that flashed on and off like faulty light bulbs. Niceness laid a sugary scent on the air as if to mitigate the fizz of barely submerged aggression. Let nobody say Americans aren't *nice*. It's in the genes, a reflex.

Perhaps it was just 42nd Street that was this way because it was a roughhouse place back then and may still be for all I know. Surely the whole of New York couldn't be so weird? Nobody looked twice at a big black guy roller-skating backwards – *backwards!* – down the road with a tin-foil hat on his head, weaving through the traffic in a dare-devil performance that made me yearn to ask him: why?

If you are normal you can't help but slap yourself to make sure you are awake, buy a hot-dog from the street vendor (easy on the ketchup) and give a yell for the magnificence of being alive, knowing you will not raise a flicker of interest because nobody gives a damn about you. You simply have to be in love at first sight with the place, or you have no blood. There'll be time enough to hate it if you must, which many do, but I never did. There were still places to see with names that had run around our heads for half our lives:

Brooklyn, the Bronx, Queens, Staten Island, Times Square. But this was enough sensory attack for now.

I went to work next day at the office on Third Avenue and looked out of the window high up in the sky and there it was, down there, my playground. The great thing about the New York job was that I travelled most of the time, because even New York couldn't produce enough news by itself. And so I got to see every part of America save Hawaii and Alaska, but before that happened there were other priorities, like finding a home. After the first day in Manhattan it was clear to Valerie and me that we couldn't live in the city, because we were naïve enough to let our two little girls pop downstairs to get an ice-cream from the shop by the hotel and straight away a man chatted them up. Big sister Melanie had the good sense to lead herself and Maria straight back upstairs. I charged down to commit murder, but he had gone.

'You let them do what? By themselves?' The office secretary was aghast. And so we rented a suburban house across the river in a place called Teaneck, New Jersey, and the house turned out to be criminally awful, a testament to cover-up and lies when we had briefly inspected it with a real estate agent before signing the rental agreement. There was no hot water, no central heating, terrible plumbing, and we had to threaten to sue the landlord and the realtors to release us from the agreement and give our deposit back.

We were nearly a couple of months into America by now and unsettled by a sense of homelessness. We had no car and possessed nothing we couldn't carry in suitcases from

England, giving us a sense of what it's like to be immigrants. But of course we weren't jobless and had somewhere to go home to if things didn't work out. Not to mention comprehensive health insurance, which defines much of life – rather literally – in America. You ain't got it, you die.

As we walked back to that ghastly house with the kids from the supermarket one Saturday, feeling despondent, it rained and the paper bags spewed everything over the pavement. It felt like the last straw. A stranger pulled up, said we seemed to have a problem, and had a good laugh at our predicament. He popped the boot, helped us pile everything in, drove us to the house, helped us unload and drove away. Just like that. 'Y'all have a nice day now!' Our spirits rose.

We found another house in a nearby place called Bogota, which we bought. The neighbour, a big-bellied man who was never out of vest and braces, loaned us one of his two cars, an enormous Chevy that had a monstrous engine beneath a bonnet big enough for a helipad. Imagine such generosity to a couple of complete strangers. Big-hearted, big-bellied America had embraced us and everything was going to be fine. Valerie did the moving alone, because I had raced off.

Argentina had invaded the Falkland Islands.

I booked a flight to Buenos Aires without going home. I always had my passport with me – as a plumber carries a wrench, so to speak. Like most people I had to check where the Falklands were, because they sounded Scottish. In Buenos Aires I presented my passport rather nervously at

the immigration booth because the entry of British journal-
ists had been restricted.

'Are you here to cover the liberation of the Malvinas?'

'The what? Sorry, I don't know what you mean.'

'Are you a journalist?'

'Me? No, certainly not. I'm here on business for Barclays
Bank.'

He seemed about to ask for proof of occupation, but then
stamped me in with a look that said he wasn't fooled for a
minute. I almost danced out of the airport, knowing that
one of the biggest stories in the world at that time awaited
me.

I stayed at the Sheraton Hotel, where most of the dozen
or so British press corps eventually holed up, monitoring
with the aid of a translator the slide into war and the wildly
optimistic mood of the nation. The only way to file copy
was to dictate it to the copytakers in London from the hotel
telephone at ruinous expense, and the bill when I left was
42,000 US dollars – not including the room. People used to
listen in as I was dictating copy and once somebody butted
in and said, 'I'm going to get you, English bastard.'

Victory over the impending British counter-invasion
was certain because the military dictatorship said so, and
right to the end the Argentine media obediently stuck to
this line. Nobody had previously cared a hoot about the
Islas Malvinas stuck out in the misery of the Atlantic with
lots of depressed sheep and inhabited by mad people who
chose to live there. But a concerted propaganda campaign
had pummelled people into caring. Posters showing a

bullet-holed Union Jack appeared all over Buenos Aires, and late one night I took one down from inside a bus shelter to keep as a memento. It hangs in a frame on my wall to this day. Impending defeat eventually forced its way through the propaganda cracks as the war progressed, but ordinary people were never any less than cordial to us Brits.

That attitude made it harder to bear as I watched the body bags being brought ashore from the *Belgrano*, an Argentinian warship from which 323 lives were lost after it was sunk by a British submarine close to the Falkland Islands. I saw the stricken relatives standing huddled together and all my Belfast experiences came welling up and I didn't know what to think about it. Some said the *Belgrano* was steaming away from the conflict and posed no harm; others insisted it was repositioning itself for attack, which subsequent evidence has supported. I was so distressed by the body-bags I had a rant at the Foreign Desk in London, just letting off steam, and before I knew it the editor – Charles Douglas-Home by now – was on the phone asking if I wanted to be relieved of the story. Not a chance. I carried on.

I routinely sounded out local opinion in a bar called Bar Sedons, and as I left there one night I was bundled into a police car. As I was driven round the city an earnest conversation was conducted over the police radio. Two pairs of eyes regularly looked back at me through the glass partition and the glum expressions were not encouraging. I knew all about 'disappearances' in Argentina. And then we were back outside Bar Sedons, the door was opened and I was deposited back onto the pavement precisely where they had picked me up. I suppose I came close to something unpleasant that day.

The Argentine military kept a tight control on street protests, but every now and then one would erupt in the big plaza outside the Casa Rosada, the pink palace dear to the Argentine psyche because Eva Peron delivered spellbinding speeches from its balconies. Most of the protests were organised by relatives who wanted to know the whereabouts of brothers, sons and husbands snatched into oblivion by the military dictatorship. In one such demonstration I was doing some street interviews when I noticed a soldier staring at me, and suddenly he lifted his teargas riot gun and fired a canister at my head. I flinched and the canister passed over my shoulder, close enough to feel it go by. It would have killed me.

Three British journalists turned up at the hotel in a terrible state late one evening after being missing the whole day. They had been picked up on the streets as I had been, but in their case by non-uniformed security police who drove them into the countryside where they were ordered to strip naked and walk down a dirt track. They were expecting to be shot, but then the vehicle drove off, with their clothes inside. There they stood, naked, penniless, not a soul anywhere around. They walked down the track until they spotted a farmer on a tractor, who gave them sacking to wrap round themselves, and in due course they made their way back to the Sheraton wearing clothes that kindly people had given them. The experience shook the livers out of them. Quite why anybody thought this escapade was a good idea is anybody's guess.

I filed for the front page practically every day as the war went on, plus an inside story that was meant to be a lighter read. Every night I received a telex saying something like: 'Your story leading paper. Inside piece leads page five.' You can't get a high from any substance that equals that.

There was real camaraderie between a group of us from the British press, namely the *Daily Mirror,* the *Daily Express*, the *Evening Standard,* the *Daily Telegraph,* the *Daily Mail* and the *News of the World.* We got to calling each other Bill, which was a strange kind of bonding.

The man from the *Mail* moved in with a local woman but dropped by the hotel all the time to see us. He went back to his wife and kids when the war was over. The *Telegraph* man was an old pro who had covered the Vietnam war and lived with a Vietnamese girl during much of it, all but forgetting he had a wife and kids back home. He said he found normal life difficult and that his family were always trying to get him to drink less. The man from the *Mirror* ended up as its editor, but in Buenos Aires he was merely the chap called Noddy because when he got drunk he nodded like a spring-loaded toy until his head reached the table.

The *Daily Express* chap was nicknamed Brenda, the Private Eye name for the Queen, because he had hair as tall as hers. The guy from the *News of the World* had a column in the paper called Plain John Smith, which allowed him to go all over the world doing stories that took his fancy. He once spent an entire day on a camel travelling through a desert in the Middle East so he could start his column with 'I spent last night in a town called Tit.'

When I left Argentina after three months I arranged to meet Valerie in Barbados. The flight went via Venezuela so I took the chance to sniff around Caracas for a few days. On the plane I talked to a delightful Venezuelan woman who warned me how dangerous the city could be, and as her brother was collecting her from the airport she would be delighted to give me a ride into town. I accepted gratefully. And she could recommend a terrific hotel where I could stay for a song because she knew the manager. What nice people these Venezuelans were!

I was in their car heading to the hotel when alarm bells rang, because the 'brother' bore no resemblance to his 'sister,' and the snatched looks between them were not sibling-like. I was checking into the hotel, which was extremely basic, while the woman watched me, smiling rather ostenta-tiously. Her companion, meanwhile, was off somewhere. And suddenly my instincts shouted at me. I picked up my bag, literally ran to the door and hurtled down the street just as the 'brother' was turning up in a car with two other men. They bounded after me, but the streets were crowded and I got away. I suppose kidnapping a Western journalist was in their minds. Half a minute more of hesitation and I would have been in line for another big adventure. I found somewhere to stay for a few days and headed for Barbados, where Valerie and I had a week to ourselves.

We went home to a delirious welcome from our children, who were staying with a newly-found friend of Valerie's. I was amazed when I walked into our house in Bogota. This really was ours? We owned it, sort of? We had bought it with a 105 per cent mortgage – we just asked and the bank gave it to us. America, what a place! I had only ever seen the house briefly and had little memory of what it was like, and to be honest it was rather dog-eared. Valerie had bought most of the furniture because the owners were downsizing to a Florida apartment, and at last we now had firm roots, with kids in school, our own furnished home, and very soon our own car in the drive. We returned the Chevy to our big-bellied friend next door. It was now time to start plotting story ideas that would take me all over America. First, however, I began with a New York story.

There is a jail on an island in the middle of the East River, between Queens and The Bronx, called Rikers Island, one of the world's biggest prisons. It is the main complex in New York City for holding people awaiting trial for rape, murder and armed robbery. Few who end up there could afford lawyers, so they rotted for years at the mercy of state-supplied defence attorneys and a judicial system too crowded, cynical and incompetent to cope. It was brutal in there. Nobody left the same as they went in.

The prison authorities surprisingly granted my request to visit. Every second I was in there I imagined not being able to leave: to have to spend a whole night in it, a week, a month, was unthinkable. It was a stinking, rat-infested, cockroach-ridden hellhole where inmates fell into two categories: predator and prey. For some, incarceration in this place was slow psychological death, and not so slow for those who succumbed to the Rikers tradition of suicide.

The clanking of iron doors, the echo of yelling men, the smell of disinfectant and urine, the sound of demonstrably mentally ill men screaming at nothing for hour after hour, guards swinging clubs and yelling orders as if at disobedient dogs: it was a world of horrors. Prisoners called it 'Torture Island' and 'The Oven' because of the killer summer heat. For brutality and inhumanity, it had no Western rival. It has long been earmarked for closure. It once contained 20,000 prisoners packed like battery hens; nowadays it has 7,000, still beyond humane levels.

Back then, as now, inmates died at the hands of other inmates and guards would beat prisoners senseless. Drugs were ubiquitous, rape commonplace. It produced lots of horror stories, including one about a boy sent there aged 16 accused of stealing a backpack; after six years awaiting trial he killed himself. Half the time he was in solitary confinement, a cell of white tiles, a single sink, a lavatory in a corner, an iron-framed bed and a window too small to admit more than token light. These places were assuredly designed to destroy people. I stood inside one of those cells, briefly empty awaiting its next tenant, and felt the fear as clearly as a hand on my shoulder. Nowadays nobody under 18 is sent to Rikers. Most inmates eventually pleaded guilty, even if they were innocent, so they could go to trial and cut a deal for a lighter sentence. Around 90 per cent of prisoners eventually did this. I was shown around the black section of the prison. Whites and Hispanics were kept elsewhere. Blacks and Hispanics are devoted enemies and must be kept apart. Whites have no friends except each other and had their own wing, although there were few of them. It was essentially a jail for blacks and browns. The toughest of the tough were pumping iron while the second tier in the hier-archy looked on awaiting their turn. The venomous looks in my direction thankfully came from the other side of iron bars. These were bloodied men, and some looked pathologi-cally mad. Years of being caged up here and elsewhere made many of them unfit for life outside – brutal and brutalised, snarling through the cages, muscles and veins bulging from weight-lifting. One day inside it left me sleepless for a week.

South Dakota is big and it's empty: almost the size of England, but with millions fewer people. I drove through its plains and prairies for hours, passing through occasional little places with haphazard clapboard houses, a diner and a gas station, and the inevitable hardware store. I was on my way to the Oglala Sioux Indian reservation, Pine Ridge. I could imagine herds of buffalo roaming around those vast spaces before ten million were slaughtered to starve the Indians, but nothing moved out there now, save breezes in the grass. I stopped the car to listen. Few places are so silent and empty, as if the world had ended.

A sign on the roadside finally said I was entering the Oglala reservation, and not long afterwards Pine Ridge rose out of the horizon. It was hideous, a rural ghetto. Haggard whiskered men were slumped in chairs outside decrepit trail-er-homes, piles of crumpled beer-cans at their side. Old cars, mattresses and fridges littered the place and the corrugated tin roofs of slum huts were held down with rocks. Groups of drunks leaned on lamp posts, not surly, not anything. People glanced at me indifferently: just another white man poking around. One in four children here was born with foetal alcohol syndrome. Alcoholism was close to 90 per cent and unemployment was a whisker shy of 100 per cent. The destruction of these people was absolute, a place of the walking dead.

I was there to do a background feature about a legal battle for ownership of the Black Hills, which belonged to the Sioux Nation under a treaty of 1868 but were stolen by the government when gold was discovered. A certain Lieutenant Colonel Custer headed the mining expedition that made this discovery. His comeuppance came at the Little Big Horn, a battle known to Indians as the Battle of the Greasy Grass. Most of us know it as Custer's Last Stand. The Indians were later massacred for that victory.

One of the lawyers in the Black Hills case, a Sioux himself, walked me around the litter-strewn streets. 'See what they did to us?' he said, pointing to the drunks and dilapidation. 'They broke our hearts, smashed us, stole our lands, our culture, our self-respect. All we have left is drink.' This sorry place was home to 20,000 people and was the poorest of all Indian reservations. Life expectancy was 46 for men, 52 for women.

Saturday night passed with lots of dancing and singing under the stars, and it sounded like a war dance from a Hollywood movie. I was invited to one of these parties and was warmly welcomed by all. Despite the booze nobody was in the least menacing, just a lot of hollow men and women shouting at nothing much.

The Deep South carries the anguish of its music: a melancholy place, vastly empty, vastly poor, hot and humid, agonising over itself all the time, the Blues always pumping out of radio stations to keep the pain fresh. There were lots of cotton fields in places I visited, and they exuded a poignancy as strong as any historic building. I stopped at a quiet field and tried my hand at a task indelibly associated with the Old South. With the very first pluck at a cotton-ball I learned the truth of what they sing about: those needles dig deep if you don't do it right.

I sat on the porch of a wooden hut with a black woman who looked and sounded like Mammy from *Gone With The Wind*, complete with headscarf, and she related astonishing stories of her childhood. She remembered lynchings and Ku Klux Klan raids, and recalled the fatal danger of stepping out of line in those not-so-far-off times. She now lived alone in the hut on nothing but food stamps and charity. She laughed with all her copious body, shaking from head to foot, a raucous affirmation that she had not given up on life.

I was down there to do a series of articles about the Deep South during a presidential election campaign. Everywhere, on all sides, white and black, attitudes were hard and old, rusted solid by time. It was said that whites still voted the way their daddy shot in the Civil War.

In Alabama I went to a Ku Klux Klan rally. Hundreds of people wandered around in white capes and pointy hoods and I was approached by people wanting to know why I wasn't in uniform. I told them honestly, expecting to be expelled, but nobody seemed to mind and were happy to show me around and teach me the truth. A friendlier bunch you couldn't imagine.

In the middle of this gathering was a large cross, perhaps 30 feet high, crafted out of entire tree trunks. After dark it was set alight amid a roar of approval. There was a big police presence, but they kept to the sidelines and didn't interfere. As the cross burned out and the proceedings began to wind down I was approached by a Wizard in the KKK hierarchy. His wife was with him, carrying an infant looking cute in a pointy KKK hood. He asked me what I thought of it all.

I told him I found it sick.

'Huh?'

'Sick.'

He opened his cape and displayed a handgun.

'What?' he said.

A policeman hustled up, took me by the arm, escorted me to a patrol car and drove me away. 'You don't know what you're messing with,' he said. 'Get the fuck out and stay out.' I was happy with that.

I was in Dallas and decided to knock off a totally unresearched, frivolous piece about the city's bitter rivalry with Houston. It ran on the back page under a 'Letter From Dallas' headline, and I thought no more about it until it got quoted all over the Dallas newspapers. I had merely offered a layman's impression that Dallas had the edge over Houston in architecture, culture and the people. To be honest, I had no idea what I was talking about.

Next thing I knew I got invited to the annual Dallas Ball which the state government threw for itself, in which it handed out various awards. I got awarded the Freedom of the City, and I still have the certificate on my wall to prove it. I was escorted to this occasion from the airport in a Rolls Royce, accompanied by two gorgeous and impeccably well-behaved young women who did this kind of thing for a living on behalf of the city administration. The night before the Ball they took me out in the Rolls-Royce for a bar-crawl, and we ended up in a place called the J R Ewing Bar – named after the star in the blockbuster TV series *Dallas*. It amazed me that everybody was a woman, until it dawned me that this was a transvestite bar. It was my companions' idea of a joke on this innocent Englishman. The day after the Ball they took me to a barbecue lunch at the palace-sized ranch where *Dallas* was filmed. It was all a rather giddy experience.

Canada is rarely in the news radar. I only ever went there for general elections and big weather stories, because nothing else about the country stirred any interest back in London. It's no surprise that 90 per cent of the population live within 100 miles of the American border: everything else is snow and mosquitoes.

But in 1982 it burst onto the world's front pages when the *Ocean Ranger*, an offshore drilling rig, sank in the Grand Banks of Newfoundland and all 84 crew perished. I went to St Johns, the closest town. It was February. Snow blowers had created snow-mountains high as two houses on both sides of the roads and it was snowing still. I couldn't imagine how the native Indians of yore survived such elements: half the year covered in snow, the other half covered in mosquito bites. I was told it was commonplace to cake themselves in mud at the height of the mosquito season, when even wild animals were driven mad.

I attended a press conference given by the rig owners, Mobil, at which we were told how many had died and the known circumstances of the disaster. I rushed off to find a payphone to file to London, but half way through dictating I had to stop and get back into the car or turn to ice. I dictated the rest ten minutes later. And people chose to live there?

CHAPTER EIGHT

It was 5am and the foreign editor was on the line from London, dragging me out of bed at home in Washington (we had by now been transferred from New York) to tell me in a rather excited way that Maurice Bishop had been murdered. I was suitably astonished. Fuck me, I said. Bloody hell. I was told to get there fast as I could and I said I was already on the way. Trouble is, I had never heard of Maurice Bishop and had no idea where I was supposed to go.

I twiddled the radio dial in search of news bulletins and learned that he was prime minister of Grenada and that early reports suggested Cuban-backed communist insurgents had killed him. I thought Granada was in Spain, but this other one was an island in the Caribbean spelled differently. So that was the story: communists in America's back yard. Hot news.

I flew to Barbados and pondered how to get to Grenada,

because the airport had been closed by whoever was now in charge. America already had warships on the way and there were rumours it was planning a full-scale invasion to drive the enemy out. Had the Cubans really meddled in Grenada? Did they actually have troops on the ground? Were they that stupid? Would mighty America really storm this gnat-sized island?

I was taking a quick lunch in downtown Georgetown, the Barbados capital, and in one of those weird coincidences I got chatting to a fellow foreigner at the bar who turned out to be a military-related diplomat at the US embassy. I let him know I was a White House accredited correspondent and he quietly informed me that American troops were already landing at Barbados airport for an imminent invasion. Because of this fluke encounter I had a cracking story to tell, but first I had to confirm it.

I grabbed a taxi to the airport and, sure enough, American transport aircraft were landing. The invasion was getting under way! I filed a story from a public phone in the airport, which made the front-page splash. Within 24 hours America had sealed off Grenada and soon afterwards troops were storming ashore. It didn't take long to secure the island because there was nothing to secure – no communist storm-troopers, alas, and nothing abnormal happening on the streets.

This escapade – justified by the absurd claim that it was meant to save American tourists from the wicked Cubans – was a ruse to steer the headlines away from calamitous events in the Middle East, where dozens of soldiers had died in a suicide attack on a US base, for which the Reagan Administration was taking heavy political flak.

Journalists were not allowed to accompany US troops to Grenada because they would have discovered what a sham the invasion was. The editor in London, Charles Wilson, sent word that he wanted me to be the first journalist to get a story out of the island and he didn't care if I had to hire a submarine to do it. 'Spend whatever it takes,' I was told. This of course was pre-Internet, when newspapers had money to flaunt.

I hired a fast boat to take me to a tiny place called Union Island, 20-odd miles off the northern coast of Grenada. The boat owner refused to try landing in Grenada because the US had threatened to sink any vessel crossing their newly established exclusion zone, but I found a local man who was willing to give it a go for a fistful of dollars. We got close when a US gunboat ordered us back. We ignored their warning and pressed on. The water exploded around us with warning shots, so we turned around.

Next up, I hired a ponderous old vessel used for transporting livestock. It smelled accordingly. I thought a boat so decrepitly innocent might sneak through, but the same thing happened. The skipper had an idea, however. He knew a rum smuggler on Union Island named Hilarious. That really was his name. Hilarious had a substantial homemade boat in the shape of a canoe and it had a motor which in an earlier life had propelled a tractor. It had a long pole sticking out of it with a large propeller on the end. This vessel, I was assured, went like the wind, and it transpired that it really did. It flew at terrifying speed and threatened to throw me overboard every time it took a dolphin-like leap out of the water.

I paid Hilarious more money than he ever made from a smuggling trip and promised more if he landed me ashore. One evening we motored across the water to an outcrop of rocks a mile or two off the northern coast of Grenada and there waited for the first hint of dawn to make a dash for the shore.

We got very close when a US Black Hawk helicopter – big as a house – headed towards us. It hovered above us, making a raging racket. A couple of US military men waved furiously for us to turn back, but the lure of lucre and my furious exhortations drove Hilarious on. The helicopter came down low, moved from side to side, rocked the boat and sank it. The downdraught practically tore my hair out. We were perhaps 50 yards offshore and I managed to hold onto my small suitcase as I made for land. The most precious items inside it survived dry and intact inside a big leather wallet: money, credit cards and my passport. I would have drowned rather than let go of that lot.

Troops from the 82nd Airborne ordered me face down into the sand. 'Habla ingles?' one asked, absurdly thinking I might be Cuban. It sounds a bit *Boys Own* but I had blackened my face with boot polish in the hope of looking like a local. This evidently confused him. 'Yes, I speak it quite well thank you,' I replied with an exaggerated Prince Charles accent. And he shouted, 'Fucking hell I've got a Brit.' Hilarious was taken off somewhere while the helicopter carried me to a makeshift military headquarters towards the south of the island. The doors were open on both sides and there was an alarming pull of gravity whenever we banked. The soldiers, unfazed by this, wouldn't talk to me.

After we landed and I established my identity, I got a furious bollocking from a military officer. 'My men saw you coming and they had every authority to shoot you, but they radioed for a chopper. You're lucky not to be at the bottom of the ocean.'

I had now dried out from my dunking. I was released after being told there were no telex lines, no transportation links off the island, no way of filing a story. Clear off and be careful of Cuban snipers. There weren't any, as it turned out, so that was never a problem. I found my way to St George, the capital, checked into a hotel and plotted how to file. I was the only foreign newspaperman in town, and that could not be allowed to go to waste.

For a whole day I moved around, milling with people, listening, picking up colour and background, and discovering very quickly that the idea of saving American tourists was complete nonsense. I never saw a single Cuban and neither had anybody else seen one, at least not in uniform. I had a cracking tale to tell but no way to get it out. Until, that is, I saw a ship called the *Geestport*, which was flying the British ensign. It travelled constantly around the Caribbean's Windward Islands collecting bananas and transporting them to Britain.

You needed a pass to get into the docks, so I waited for the guard to go for a pee and dashed through. I found the skipper, a Geordie, and told him my dilemma. Did he have any facility that would enable me to send a story to London? Yes, he did and yes I could use it, but it was expensive. I could have hugged him. It was a new system called Inmarsat (International Marine Satellite), and from the communications room I dictated my story to the copytakers in London and carried on doing so for three more days until the ship left. I paid him with a personal cheque. After that I was once again stranded without communications and didn't file for several days until the Americans lifted their embargo and telex lines were restored.

By the time I filed my first story from the *Geestport* I had been out of touch with London for several days, and there was concern I might indeed be at the bottom of the ocean. The foreign editor telephoned Valerie in Washington and, she recalled, talked to her in a very soft voice like they do on the television news when there's been a tragedy. Chris, he said, is missing. Last news of him was that he was heading for Grenada in some boat. Valerie, who was not a worrier, told the foreign editor not to be concerned because I would turn up eventually with a story to tell. He had called to reassure her, but it ended up the other way round.

I stayed in Grenada for several weeks and rented a small flat on the beach. The only way of communicating with London was by telex, so I talked to the office once a day through cryptic telex-ese. I established myself now and then in a bar/restaurant called the Red Lobster, which was run by a Brit who was sick of the Caribbean and wanted to sell up. There was a lovely hotel up the coast called the

Secret Harbour, overlooking a private bay where big yachts bobbed but never seemed to go anywhere. I checked in there for a night most weekends and was usually the only guest, so they always put me in a suite with a four-poster bed and a balcony overlooking the bay.

After the Americans opened up the island I was able to hop back and forth to Barbados on their C-130 transporters whenever I felt like it for a change of scene – the American military is generous to the press like that. The planes are amazing beasts, loud as a thunderstorm inside. I found Hilarious and paid him for his lost boat, which came cheaper than a submarine. I had to telex London and ask them to shovel money into my bank to cover everything I had spent.

The killers of Prime Minister Maurice Bishop were rounded up and I returned later for the trial, which resulted in people being sentenced to death, later commuted to lengthy imprisonment. It transpired that army elements had overthrown Bishop in a military coup and placed him under house arrest. He was shot when he defied his confinement and led a crowd to army headquarters, threatening to overrun it. The Cubans weren't involved at all, at least not directly.

The Queen later made an official visit on the Royal Yacht *Britannia* to re-assert Britain's interest in that part of the world, and I caught up with the vessel while it was restocking in Port of Spain, Trinidad. I managed to get myself invited to a small reception on board for B-grade guests, which the Queen didn't attend. I admired a beautiful decanter in the middle of a big dining table and was told somewhat matter-of-factly by one of the crew: 'Nelson's.' But of course.

While I was taking breakfast in a café a street person walked in and landed an almighty blow on me, sending me flying. He grabbed a little money he had spotted me place in my shirt pocket and fled. I went after him and started to catch up. He stopped, flashed a knife, and I let him go. A dollar wasn't worth dying over. Next day the local paper, the Trinidad *Bomb*, boomed: 'LONDON TIMES MAN MUGGED IN PORT OF SPAIN.' They'd picked up the incident from the local police. My elbow hurt like hell from what felt like a splintered bone, and it gave occasional trouble for years afterwards.

Britannia sailed away to Grenada and I hopped ahead of it by plane so I could be waiting on the dockside when the Queen stepped ashore. The American invasion had been popular locally because it was assumed the island would be awash with American money, but Britain had opposed it and the Queen was thus booed by some in the crowd, which I mentioned in my story. Words were whispered in my ear by British officials that the Palace was upset by this. Bang went my knighthood.

The paper decided it was neglecting Latin America and I was sent down there to dig around. It was left to me to decide where I went, so I excitedly mapped out my itinerary: Costa Rica, Guatemala, Honduras, Ecuador, Guyana, Nicaragua and Suriname, because none of those countries ever got much of an airing in international news save for Nicaragua, which had a leftist government the US wanted to overthrow. By my logic they must all contain good untold stories.

I arrived in Nicaragua, my first stop, bang on time. A huge fuel storage depot was bombed to oblivion, releasing a sea of oil that covered half a small town in stinking crude. Homes were awash in it, animals floundered in it, birds beyond measure were covered in it. The economic impact on this impoverished country was immense. In a matter of seconds almost all the country's oil reserves were lost. Who could have done that?

An eye-witness described a speedboat roaring away from the scene minutes before the blast. Everything smacked of military professionalism, and given Nicaragua's parlous relations with America I stuck my neck out and speculated that it was the work of the Central Intelligence Agency.

That night I didn't sleep, wondering if I had got it disastrously wrong. Next day I listened every hour to the BBC World Service, fearful of hearing a State Department repudiation. And then it came, an unequivocal denial of any CIA involvement whatsoever. Oh Christ.

But various news outlets in Washington soon started producing stories that challenged this official line and finally the Americans admitted that it was indeed the CIA's hand-iwork. Whether the initial statement was a cock-up or a lie I don't know.

How many years did it take to clean up those millions of litres of oil? How great was the heightened suffering of millions of poor people? What enduring damage was inflicted on the earth, the wildlife, the river, the fish, the trees? The attack was out of the news in 72 hours but the people would have lived with the aftermath for years. Those old Belfast questions arose: what was the point, what did it achieve?

And so to Suriname, the smallest country in South America, whose half a million inhabitants live mostly on or near the coast because almost everywhere else is jungle. It had hardly ever figured in the news save for a little flurry after a military coup in 1980.

I met people as discreetly as possible, having entered the country on a tourist visa because it's always better to be incognito. And right in front of my nose, just begging to be told, was a terrific story that made the front page and prompted questions at the daily State Department press briefing in Washington. The story was that the Libyan dictator Colonel Gaddafi had established a team of military advisers in the country, representing his first political foray into South America. The idea of the hated Gaddafi dabbling in America's sphere of influence sent up a howl of outrage in Washington, but not initially. To my dismay the State Department said it had no knowledge of a Libyan presence in Suriname. Oh Christ – again. But a few hours later it withdrew the denial and confirmed that it had indeed acquired intelligence reports of Libya's military meddling. In the context of Washington politics at the time, it was a major story. In the context of my career, it was a major relief.

I later learned that there had been a kerfuffle at *The Times* when the initial denial came through, and no doubt my name was mud. Indeed, the first edition of the next day's paper carried the State Department's put-down of this much-vaunted 'exclusive,' only to replace it with a confirmation story in subsequent editions. I remembered the story of an editor who cabled a foreign correspondent thus: 'Congratulations your front-page exclusive two days ago. Why still exclusive?' That's one way of sacking somebody. I thought I might get something similar.

The editor sent word that I should go into the jungle and find some Libyans. Seriously? Well yes, apparently he was, but he was easily persuaded that it was a bonkers idea. And then I got a phone call in my hotel from the person who had given me the story. 'Get out,' he said. 'Don't ask. Just leave.' I had pissed off some nasty people.

I went immediately to the airport and bought a ticket, but then I was taken aside by security personnel and escorted to a room without furniture. The plane was on the runway but wasn't being allowed to leave (it was going to Trinidad, the first flight going anywhere). Nobody came to interrogate me. A couple of people came into the room, silently took my bag apart and examined my notebooks. My bag was taken away and then returned to me, intact.

Then, without a word of explanation or a single question ever being asked, I was walked to the aircraft and shown aboard. They had held the plane for a considerable time – a couple of hours I suppose – while all this went on and the passengers stared at me as two uniformed men led me aboard. I was shaking. It was a delicious feeling as the plane left the tarmac.

The pilot came back to talk to me and asked what the

hell had happened back there. He had overheard arguments between officials over whether I should be detained or released. 'You're damned lucky,' he said. 'You really don't know how lucky you are.'

I had a ton of information in my notebooks, enough for several more stories, all of it written in shorthand, which had confounded the officials back at the airport. I checked into a hotel in Trinidad and filed four more stories on successive days with Suriname datelines.

I turned up a bunch of stories in all the other countries, spending a week to ten days in each. Honduras was stunning for its poverty. Guatemala was being brutally ruled by a military dictatorship. El Salvador was at war with itself. In Ecuador I drove to the Equator, which was marked out by a simple white line painted across a quiet rural road. One step into the northern hemisphere; one step back into the south. What fun!

Guyana was the last on my list. I was walking through a park in central Georgetown, the capital, and was startled to see a purple-painted coffin under a tree, sitting atop a refrigeration device driven by a generator. I was even more startled to discover that it had until recently contained the body of the newly deceased President Linden Forbes, whose favourite colour was purple. The generator kept breaking down and he was in rather bad shape, so they had shipped him to Moscow to be embalmed. The idea was to return him to the glass-topped coffin for permanent display, but it was a cockamamie idea from the outset and never happened. They brought him back from Moscow before the embalming was completed and mercifully buried what remained of him. It was a macabre end to my fling around South America.

I was based in Washington for the last six of my eight years in America. Val and I bought a small house in Potomac, Maryland, in the middle of a jungle of houses with fenceless front lawns and streets without pavements because there was nowhere to walk to. No parks, no shops, no bars, no restaurants: the nearest supermarket was eight sets of traffic lights away. Cutting the front lawn helped people recognise their neighbours and wave, but that's as close as you got.

Val became a real estate agent and was magnificently useless at it. One time she used her considerable people skills to talk a couple into staying together rather than splitting up, thus losing a fat commission from the sale of their house. On another occasion I came back from a trip to find our garage full of a family's possessions because they couldn't afford storage for the couple of weeks it was going to take them to move house. After a few years she gave it up, having sold precisely two houses, and went off to study for an MA in English Literature at Maryland University. She was rather better at that. She got a first.

Washington can stifle a journalist. A mountain of information has to be sifted and it kills the instincts: why try to gather information by yourself when rivers of it flow ceaselessly at you? It comes from all the major US newspapers and television stations, from screeds of press releases arriving all day long from every department of government, from the daily

State Department and White House press conferences, plus another dozen or more press conferences every day from various government agencies and lobby groups.

American newspapers are something to behold, and going through them was hard labour. A story might run on page one for 800 words, continue on page 14 for a another 600, migrate to page 26 for a few columns and die of exhaustion at the bottom of page 34. The Sunday newspapers were a 20-pound slab of depleted forest wrapped in plastic, within which were the news section, sports section, business section, week-in-review section, the colour magazine, fashion section, life-style section, travel section, metro section, classified advertisements section, the book review supplement, the theatre section, the food section, the entertainment section... about the length of six novels in one edition.

I wasn't long in Washington before I fell prey to the national obsession with litigation. A popular bumper sticker summed it up: 'Hit me, I need the money.' A neighbour's little boy fell off his bicycle in our front yard and hurt himself, and before long lawyers were baying for thousands in damages. People with tape measures and cameras came round and gravely inspected the driveway for a bump or crack that could prove negligence on my part. This got my dander up and I did a piece about it:

> If little Johnny must fall and get two stitches he should do it at nursery school because the damages will help him through college. When a doctor makes

a mistake, patients can dream of early retirement. Accountants, contractors, real estate agents, police officers, child care centres, nurses, midwives, doctors, shopkeepers, hotels, the ordinary guy in the street and lawyers themselves live in the menacing shadow of a species of attorney known as the contingency lawyer. You could pay off the mortgage if you broke a leg on an ice rink. Babysitters are eminently suable if baby Jane bumps her head. Anybody working with children had better watch out because lawyers have found mileage from the vicious term 'too much affection'.

I constantly pitched story ideas to London that would get me out of town and away from Washington politics, and once I was on the road I'd do my best to find more stories to keep me travelling. Down in Texas, ostensibly for other stuff, I tacked on an extra day to do a piece about the Alamo, which seemed rather over-blown in the historical scheme of things. But America has to cling to what little history it's got. I kicked it off like this:

> It is 97 degrees, a brutal spring day even for south Texas. The bleached-white walls of the mission San Antonio De Valero are hot as coals. It is cool inside where the Daughters of the Republic of Texas show off a couple of Davy Crockett's rifles and a collection of old Colts and Winchesters. This is a shrine, a place revered in the romance and legend of Texas. This is the Alamo, where Texas had its Mafeking

and 187 Americans died fighting for their state's independence from Mexico in 1836. It is crumbling very slowly into dust.

It is of dubious historical authenticity. Nobody tells you that the chapel, the principal building, has had ten new roofs or that the famous façade did not exist when the place was a Christian Mission. That particular adornment was built by the US Army when it turned the place into a fort. The building that houses the museum came along in the 1930s as part of a public works programme during the Depression, although there is no sign telling you so. The decay of the little that remains of the old structure eats at the very heart of a state so totally enraptured by itself and its history.

I went to Pennsylvania to have a look at the Amish. They are an insular group locked in another time, living in, but not part of, American society, totalling around 12,000 people descended from a small number who came from Europe 200-odd years earlier. Nowadays they are mostly farmers working some of the finest farmland in America. All were extremely gracious when I approached, but none wanted to talk, preferring to stay aloof from outside interaction. They would say 'God Bless You' and turn away, clopping away in horse-drawn buggies, because they never owned cars or other avoidable modern conveniences. I hung around a small town called Paradise, observing them and trying to fathom what it must be like to live with such entrenched and immutable certainties; to be always a stranger to the world around you. I kicked off my piece on a more practical note:

> From the grime and smoke-stacks of Philadelphia it is an hour to Paradise. The countryside is rich and under plough for tobacco and corn. Amish families ride by in horse-drawn buggies, eyes averted. The men have long tangled beards. The women wear baggy clothes without zips or buttons, which are not allowed. They talk quietly in Old German. At home there is no television, no electricity, no radio, telephone or books save for the Bible. Lighting is by kerosene, heating by wood stove. In the garage there is a horse-drawn buggy, never a car.

Being able to gad around an enormous continent doing these kinds of stories gave me a delicious sense of freedom. Being out there alone, finding the ideas, getting to the story, doing the interviews, forming an opinion, writing it up – it's a buzz.

The Washington bureau had two news journalists and one locally-hired economics correspondent. I was the number two, which mercifully meant I didn't do much of the big political stuff and was thus liberated to go travelling. I did get to interview President Reagan in the Oval Office of the White House, however. In those 30 minutes I tried to take in every detail and lock it in my mind, because this was never going to happen again. I noted the president's shiny black shoes, the shape of the room, the pattern on the carpet, the Rose Garden outside the window, the big desk that had seen so much history, the pen and holder on one corner of it, the clock above the fireplace. Reagan was charming but uncertain of himself, and kept turning to his aides for reassurance. He was so nice I wanted to invite him home to tea.

I followed him around the country on his campaign for re-election to a second term, and that was an eye-opener to the banality of American politics. I never knew democracy needed 10,000 balloons, five miles of bunting and a full orchestra at every stop. I went to every corner of the country on the press plane, which followed Air Force One, and it was gruelling – a quick dash into one hyped-up rally after another, ferried by bus from the plane to the venue and back in an hour or two, listening to the same speech six times a day. Now and then small groups of us would be allowed to get up close to the president on Air Force One but otherwise we were held in the background of this over-staged shebang. When the campaign ended Reagan told a group of reporters he was so sick of his own speech he wanted to burn it 'like a mortgage.' I would have done it for him.

CHAPTER NINE

'Do you want the India posting?'

'Yes.'

'It's yours.'

Click.

I was in the Washington office when these eight life-changing words came through from Charles Wilson, the editor. I was to be South Asia Correspondent covering Sri Lanka, Pakistan, Afghanistan, Bhutan, Bangladesh, Nepal, the Maldives and India itself. I would also make forays into Australia, Malaysia, Singapore, Thailand, Indonesia and Cambodia.

We put our house up for rental, gave away our old car, and in a month we were off. Leaving was tough for Val after eight years setting down roots in America, and it was a terrible wrench for ten-year-old Matthew, whose identity and accent were entirely American. The girls were at boarding school in England, so leaving wasn't such a big deal for them. I was the only one truly celebrating. 'Goodbye America,' I crassly said as the plane took off from Dulles Airport. Matthew and Valerie dissolved into tears.

It was June. The monsoon was about to inflict its vital annual misery when we landed in Delhi beneath a black and angry sky. We handed the man at the customs desk a bulging file of paperwork we had assembled for our dog, which he handed back without looking at it. 'Dog,' he observed astutely, casting an eye at a cage containing our hysterically emotional border collie, Jamie.

Heat and 90 per cent humidity hammered us as we walked out of the airport, and far-off thunder created a sense of approaching drama. We were instantly hit by the mayhem of the mob. Porters fought for our suitcases, taxi touts tugged, beggar children swarmed, the whole world shoved and shouted as we fought through the melee looking for the man who was supposed to meet us, but he wasn't there because it's law in India to be late.

We found him, rammed our suitcases into the car and headed to our new home through Delhi's traffic madness. The law of the road was immediately apparent: size counts. People moved for bicycles, bicycles for scooters, scooters for motorcycles, motorcycles for cars, cars for buses, buses for trucks, trucks for nobody. Unless there was a cow in the road. Everybody moved for a holy cow.

We reached our soon-to-be-home suburb, Kailash Colony, and paused to take in the local market as we drove by. There were a dozen or more stalls abundant with fruit and vegetables. A barber with a cracked mirror tied onto a telegraph pole shaved a man seated on a wooden stool. Hump-backed cows munched discarded rotten vegetables, the smell competing for airspace with a spice shop. Scooter rickshaws were lined up three deep. Several *dhobis* – laundrymen – worked with coal-filled irons the size of three house bricks. Ragged tarpaulins attached to the sides of buildings housed entire families. Amid all this poverty, a swanky jewellery shop sold 22-carat gold. This was our introduction to the economic contrasts of India: severe and sublime at each end, and not much in the middle.

Home at last to a monstrously big, flat-roofed house inherited from my predecessor. I was taken aback to be called *sahib*. Valerie was *memsahib*, although the cleaner called her 'sir.' Matthew was *chota-sahib*, little boss. It came with a cast of characters: cook, dhobi, chowkidars (guards), mali (gardener), bearer (cleaner), driver/messenger and very soon a crap-collector. No caste Hindu would clear the dog's mess so we had to hire an Untouchable (otherwise known as Dalits), because excrement is their business. She came every day, a craven woman, lowest in the heap, scullion from birth to death. The difference between her fortunes and mine was the accident of birth: there is no justice to that particular stroke of bad luck. A fierce storm destroyed her squalid one-room hut and I got a new one built for her in brick. The belle of the slum.

Lal the cook was a drunk who topped up my liquor bottles with water. Dass the bearer was a prodigious thief who unscrewed the hinges of one cupboard door so often it fell out late one night with a mighty crash. Raj the driver siphoned petrol and had a deal with the local garage workshop to do phantom repairs. The dhobi nicked clothes. This pilfering was routine, unstoppable and totally understandable. Most were low-caste Hindus and a couple were Christians (which is lower still).

It's a privilege to have a phalanx of servants to take over the mundane tasks of life, but there is a high price, and that is the loss of privacy. To talk privately Val and I shut ourselves in the office and whispered. Bank statements and personal letters had to be burned because they would be discovered and studied. Phone conversations were monitored on the extension phone in the hall. The scale of intrusion was best demonstrated when somebody on the Foreign Desk phoned to talk to one of my predecessors and was told by a servant: 'Sahib is in bed, sir, on top of memsahib.'

As for the job, I didn't have a single phone number to help me on my way. Derek Brown, my equivalent on *The Guardian*, rode to the rescue and sealed our long friendship by letting me rummage through his contacts book. We travelled to Pakistan together a few times and during one of those escapades I put it to him: 'Don't you think it's amazing we're being paid to do this?' Indeed he did.

In the next ten years I dealt with bandits and brothel-keepers, fake gurus and murderous monks, Hindu extremists and Muslim madmen, Afghan warlords and Indian slum bosses, presidents and prime ministers, erstwhile maharajas, lots of villains masquerading as politicians, remote tribes of India, some quite terrifying tribal leaders of Pakistan, many magnificent souls quietly doing heroic works, and one very fine and elegant king who had four wives who were all sisters. He was King Wangchuck of Bhutan, a jewel of a country squeezed between India and China, the last of the Himalayan Buddhist kingdoms, and I couldn't believe my luck when he granted a request for an interview. He didn't normally give interviews, preferring to keep his country aloof from the world, so my request must have reached him on a good day.

Bhutan felt like Utopia. It had always contained population growth by sending at least one child from each family to monasteries or nunneries, and that meant it had a sense of space that didn't exist in most parts of teeming Asia. There were no great land-owners that I could see on a long tour of the country, no evidence of stark rich-poor divides, and the king was no despot. He submitted his powers to parliamentary scrutiny and people revered him. Corruption in all areas of life was minimal, and begging was non-existent.

The king had been educated in England until the age of 17, when he had had to return after his father died. He immediately established preservation of his country's culture and environment as his mission. He banned television, although later he granted its selective introduction, and kept tourism to strict limits.

I met him in his palace in Thimpu, the tiny capital, and he talked at length about his efforts to save the forests in the south of the country from Nepalese incursions. Whole swathes of remote woodland had been razed by hit-and-run logging, and Nepalese peasants, starved out of their own country by their abuse of it, were pouring in to farm the cleared land. He talked about the calamity of over-tourism, especially of the back-packing kind that brought more trouble than money in Nepal. He insisted that gross domestic product was not a measure of happiness.

I left my intrusive questions to the end.

'You have four wives, all sisters?'

'Yes.'

'And they all live together in your palace with your children?'

'Yes.'

'But you live in a relatively modest wooden house in the mountains, alone?'

'Yes.'

'Why?'

He stroked his chin.

'If you had four wives, wouldn't you?'

He handed me a gift of a hand-made *thanka* that included pure gold threads and was truly beautiful and alarmingly valuable. I told him I was unable to accept gifts – a house rule of *The Times*. But, he said gently, it would be greatly upsetting if I refused to accept it. So I did, and called the paper immediately I got back to Delhi to confess. Nobody cared, and it hangs on my wall still, in a glass frame.

Saturday morning, the doorbell rings at my house-cum-office. Standing on the step is a man I have never met who will tell me a remarkable story that every newspaper in

Delhi has tried to crack. He is tall and good-looking with black neatly-cut hair, his clothes are Western, his bearing aristocratic. We talk over a pot of tea. After describing his situation he invites me to see where he and his sister live. Then I will understand.

Extraordinary rumours had for years swirled around these two siblings, but they never gave interviews and had nothing to do with the outside world. They decided, however, to offer their story to *The Times* because they wanted 'the Queen of England' to know their plight and help them. Through no effort of mine, a terrific tale had simply walked up to my front door.

The pair occupied an ancient tumbledown hunting lodge in New Delhi, near the big houses and wide roads of the diplomatic quarter, tucked alongside a trail that used to be known as Mountbatten Way because that was where the last viceroy rode horses. Trees hid it from view.

I stepped into this structure up broken stone steps, and several pigeons flew out. Five huge dogs howled and strained against their restraints. The sister sat silently on a stone bench, the only seating, staring hard at me. She did not approach, did not speak, did not move. There was no television, no radio, no electricity, no heating, no cooling, no fridge, no stove, no glass in the windows. Rain, cold, heat and wind blew in freely throughout the seasons. The roof leaked. The dogs were going mad to get at me.

There were ragged carpets on the floor that would have been expensive once, and a few tattered tapestries on the wall. The sister's hair was slapped to her head, curly, long and filthy, and she declared in one of her few utterances that she had not stepped from this building in years, had not washed her hair in all that time, nor had a bath, and would not do so until their demands were met. I suppose she was mad. She was cadaverous, bones jutting out of her. Her voice shook, her clothes were old, her teeth rotten. Her brother kept looking at her affectionately. He had not gone to seed like this. He still had bearing.

These were the last two descendants of a once powerful Indian royal family, both carrying airs of grandeur and a belief that they merited rights and privileges befitting their background. The brother had written personally to the Queen, one royal to another, about his slide into penury and said he was awaiting a reply but felt an article in *The Times* would focus her attention. He had sent documents and historical manuscripts to Buckingham Palace to authenticate his story and had no doubt the Queen would soon reply. This, then, was unfolding as a story of riches to rags, power to impotence, and a slide into madness. Their forebears had been giants of their world and, from all historical accounts I could track down, most were quite pitiless towards the millions who paid obeisance to them. The siblings were the last of the former princely state of Oudh, an empire of 24,000 square miles established in 1732 and centred on what is now Uttar Pradesh, in northern India. Successive nawabs of Oudh – they were Shia Muslims – had been among the wealthiest princes in the land. The British took control of Oudh in 1856, citing corruption and misrule, which helped precipitate the 1857 Indian Mutiny.

After the seizure of Oudh the ousted royal family's fortunes began to shrink, and each generation was poorer than the last. The last two descendants were now penniless. Their mother, who they called the Begum, had died a few years earlier. They told me she had killed herself by swallowing the last diamonds she owned and that they had been kept for this express purpose – a death befitting a queen. The stones tore through her and her death was agonising. They showed me the bowl from which she had taken them and placed them into her mouth. Both had watched her die, and saw it as a glorious ending. The sister called it 'a drink of fire' and said it was a quick death. 'You must not call it that word, s-u-i-c-i-d-e,' she insisted.

For a long time they slept with the body between them. The brother told me this in a manner suggesting it was quite normal. They loved her, he explained, and didn't want her to go. The corpse was dressed in a raw silk peacock-blue sari and six months later, when it had dehydrated, he embalmed it. She was moved to a small tomb be built outside the lodge, where she remained for six more months until she was committed to the flames. The sister said I must not use that 'common word, c-r-e-m-a-t-i-o-n.'

For years the destitute Begum and her children had occupied the former waiting room of the viceroy of India at Delhi railway station, which they shared with 13 dogs and seven servants. They constantly appealed to politicians for proper accommodation and a stipend worthy of their ex-royalty. It was Indira Gandhi who, as prime minister, allocated them the derelict hunting lodge, a spiteful gesture to get them out of the railway station. They received a monthly stipend of 500 rupees, then worth about £9. I wrote:

> Deep in the Delhi woods five howling great Danes and Dobermans strain at chains anchoring them to a derelict 13th century hunting lodge – windowless, door-less, waterless and foul – where their master and mistress, impoverished hermits both, carry the Royal House of Oudh through its death throes. Deeds strange and macabre have gone on here. Princess Rajkumari Sakina Mahal lives here with her brother Prince Rajkumar Cyrus Riza in conditions that are beyond poverty. It is a deathly place filled with a constantly articulated desire by the princess and prince finally to end the humiliation of the great House of Oudh. The many palaces and legions of servants have long gone, and the remaining royals are reduced to squalor made starker by an attachment to a few threadbare carpets and some slivers of diamonds, the last of anything worthwhile. They reject an India they despise for bringing them to this.

I sent the article it to them as soon as it was published. They sent it back in shreds. It wasn't to their liking.

The madam of one of the biggest brothels in Bombay (Mumbai) was in a rage. Her immense body writhed inside trembling layers of fat, her tree-trunk arms flailed, her bulldog face snarled at the six policemen trying to arrest her. Wisely, they stood back until this giant gorgon calmed down lest they were bludgeoned senseless. When the tsunami subsided she was taken outside and heaved and tugged into a police van because she was too obese to do it alone, and I climbed in after her. Crowds gathered round, attracted by her stentorian screaming.

We sat together in silence as she sweated, panted and cursed in the terrible heat of the vehicle. Bombay traffic provided all the time in the world for her to pull herself together as we headed to the police station, and eventually she began to lighten up, even smile. She had obviously been here before. She wanted to know what the fuck I was doing in this van with her – she was efficiently foulmouthed in English as well as her native Marathi – and when I told her she laughed. A fucking reporter! She loved it. She said she would be free within an hour and didn't give a fuck who knew she bribed the police.

I had gone to the brothel to watch a police raid, of which I had prior notice. The brothel was essentially a prison for prostitutes in an area known locally as The Cages because it contained several brothels in which the girls – most were that – were displayed in iron cages like zoo animals. I turned up well before the raid to watch and wait. A few men were sitting on hard benches, sizing up the girls before making a choice. A man pointed out one of them and escorted her upstairs. The girls were mostly Nepalese because their fair skins were popular. The trade in girl-trafficking from Nepal was rampant and doubtless still is, and it worked very simply: place an advertisement in a Nepali newspaper for a domestic servant with fares paid to India, and off they go in terrible innocence, usually with the connivance of parents knowing what they were doing. Not only did they avoid future dowry; they got paid.

The police arrived at the brothel later than planned – the law of lateness – with a lot of yelling and door-slamming and wielding of the infamous *lathi*, a thick heavy cane that can inflict great physical harm. I ran up the stairs with them into a large area divided by curtains, and each partition contained a thin mattress. A tumescent man tried to pull his trousers on and was mocked and abused by the police but not arrested. He flew down the stairs, still hitching up his trousers. The supposed point of this raid was to rescue Nepali trafficked girls, but that didn't happen. It never did. It was a ruse for extracting money from the madam. The girls were village kids, nothing more, who would spend their youth in this place until they were too old – in their early twenties – and were thrown out to work the streets freelance.

There was a meagre centre in Bombay run by a charity where Nepali ex-prostitutes could live, because it was impossible to go home with such a history. For many with AIDS, this was a hospice. I went there, and it was a tragic place of women with no future but this. There was, never-theless, a warm sense of community among them, and lots of laughter. They welcomed me with a cup of *chai* and an honest discussion of their stories. They weren't self-pitying; what most troubled them were all those 14-year-olds still being put through abominable apprenticeships in The Cages and elsewhere with nobody to turn to. These women carried an unexpected serenity that came, I suppose, from knowing they were now safe. Some knew the madam I had met and they loathed her. We talked about her a lot, and she was by all accounts a brute.

The woman certainly loved to talk. Once in her stride she didn't stop to take breath while we were in the police van. She likened the girls to wild horses. 'At first they want to escape. You give them ten men a day for three months and that breaks them. They never leave after that and I can let them out onto the streets because they'll always come back. Where else would they go?'

Few places in the habitable world are colder than a midwinter night in one of Mr Butt's houseboats on Kashmir's Dal Lake. Five blankets, woolly socks, a thick vest and a double-knit sweater were not enough. The cold got into bed with you from underneath, straight out of the water. But I would never have stayed anywhere else, and that was because of the remarkable Mr Butt.

To cope with the Kashmir winter I did on occasion resort to a little earthenware fire-pot, the *kangri,* that Kashmiris tuck inside their cloaks – the unisex *pheran* – as a portable heating device. They are amazingly effective and cheap to run with a couple of little coals every few hours. One problem is that wisps of smoke make you smell like a steamship's stoker and cover you in soot. Another aggravating tendency is that you catch fire. They are best left to the initiated.

Visiting Kashmir in summer was another experience entirely. At the end of a working day it meant being able to sit on top of one of Mr Butt's house-boats drinking beer out of teapots and china cups, a necessary ruse because an alcohol ban had been imposed by separatist gunmen. From this vantage point you could watch herons and kingfishers at work and monitor the frenetic life of the lake and its shores. The lake itself was in deep trouble because tens of thousands of security forces emptied their effluent into it, but it was still an outstanding sight.

Mr Butt hosted lots of foreign correspondents on his boats because of his inexhaustible conviviality, which sometimes meant being invited to sit on the floor with his family to eat dinner finger-style. But what most impressed everybody was his resilience. He just wouldn't give up and leave Kashmir when it turned dangerous. He was always in trouble with somebody waving a gun in his face, be it a soldier or one of the young, separatist idiots who called themselves militants. He was in an impossible position: the militants threatened to kill him if he didn't give them money, and the security forces threatened to kill him if he did.

Before dawn he would send a man to heave logs into an enormous wood-burning furnace on the lakeshore next to his boats, and after an hour of smoke-belching struggle it would yield hot water. There was frequently no power for the electric heaters but they were useless anyway against the winter elements, so it was usually almost as cold inside as out. With the announcement that there was hot water I would lug the bedclothes aside, cough from the dust of ages bursting out of them, and dive for the shower.

Mr Butt had inherited the business from his father, who

used to host British army officers and government officials visiting Kashmir on holiday, as well as some who retired there rather than eke out their pensions in Bournemouth. But they were few: 'staying on,' as they called it, was acceptable in Kenya or Ceylon or Malaya, but had a peculiar stigma when it came to India.

Soldiers occupied every major street-corner of the capital, Srinagar, bored, underpaid, lonely, nervous and hated. They were unable to say anything intelligible to the local populace because they didn't speak Kashmiri. They were puny, bony-assed and not much taller than their rifles, but I am grateful to them. This is why.

The only way to send copy to London in my early forays into Kashmir before half-decent phones were introduced was by telex from the Central Telegraph Office. Kashmir was frequently – and sometimes constantly – under shoot-on-sight nightly curfews, which presented a logistical problem if you didn't get away from the telegraph office in time.

The only solution was to walk down the middle of empty ill-lit streets in defiance of the curfew shouting '*foreign press-wallah*' at jittery soldiers standing in the shadows with rifles pointed at you. None ever took a pop at me however: hence my gratitude. The man in charge of the telex office had a nice little racket going at my paper's expense. He sold my telex card details to countless people, and it took the accounts department in London a full two years to twig why the bills were so enormous.

Those long, silent walks back to Mr Butt's place were weirdly moving. It takes immense power to close down a city, silence it, turn it dark, remove its energy and confine more than a million people indoors under threat of death. Even the soldiers spoke quietly to each other during these lockdowns because they, too, felt the spell. As curfew-time approached the city would start to move and shuffle nervously, and in the final minutes it would burst into bedlam. Street traders clattered home with their carts, horse-drawn *tongas* went at a gallop, shop shutters rattled closed, the *shikara-wallahs* – the boatmen of Dal Lake – paddled off and thousands of three-wheel scooters, a curse to anything that breathes air, scattered like disturbed birds. Then, with the stroke of the hour, the city paid its silent tribute to the might of State oppression and switched off.

The point of these curfews was to thwart gangs of young gunmen who had some insane notion that they could achieve an independent Kashmir by taking on the world's second biggest army. Their word for themselves, 'militants', always vexed me: it was such a strange nomenclature used by all sides in the conflict as if by tacit agreement. Not terrorists, guerrillas, separatists, gunmen, rebels, bombers, subversives, freedom fighters or something with bite: just this limp, neutral little thing that might be describing trade union activists. It didn't convey what they did. What they did was kill. What they also did was die a lot, because they were a tragically outclassed bunch of delusional amateurs whipped up by Pakistani propaganda to fight an impossible battle.

Of course they were courageous and had every right to despise India – and Pakistan, too – but they were manipu-lated, impressionable, immature boys with an average age of 17 and with absolutely no perception of reality. The first time I met some of them was shortly after a small bomb signalled the start of the violence that continues in Kashmir to this day. It was 1989, my first year in India, and that small explosion slightly damaged the tourist office in the centre of Srinagar. I went up there to find out what was going on. Kashmir was boiling with tension.

I hadn't yet discovered Mr Butt and stayed at what was then the Oberoi Hotel, which used to be the summer palace of Kashmir's last maharajah, Hari Singh, who threw big boozy parties on the lawns overlooking Dal Lake and the Pir Panjel mountains. He liked working the barbecue, and greatly enjoyed a drink.

Five look-alike young men, bearded clones with the same jet-black hair, all wearing identical Kashmiri cloaks, strode up to the reception desk of the Oberoi and asked to see me, having heard that a foreign journalist was in town. They crowded into my room and said I should be aware that Kashmir would be independent within 12 months and I should write about it. So, I ventured, this meant that India and Pakistan would give up their rival claims to Kashmir, that the world would recognise it as an independent country, that international aid would be forthcoming to make this possible, and that you will soon be able to form a stable, democratically elected government?

They nodded excitedly. Their simplicity, their boyish enthusiasm, made me feel very sad, because they didn't know what I knew: that they were doomed.

And, I went on, practically shouting at them by now, you

think you can strut around Kashmir openly urging armed insurrection and get away with it? That you can prance into this hotel as if it lacked ears and eyes? Do you have a death wish? I admire your courage and passion and sympathise deeply with your cause, but kindly fuck off because I don't want to be responsible for what happens to you. With that, I flung open the door and ushered them out.

In due course I did meet one of the more adult leaders of this rebellion, and it was quite a palaver getting to him. I was to get into a certain taxi at a certain place and it would take me to another taxi that would take me zig-zagging all over Srinagar for a rendezvous with a 26-year-old man describing himself as commander-in-chief of the Jammu and Kashmir Liberation Front, a secessionist terrorist group – the one that started the uprising back in 1989. The meeting took place in the garden of a house surrounded by a high wall, and armed gunmen kept an eye out for any approaching soldiers as we talked. What astonished me was the man's fatal and utterly ridiculous certainties. He was no wiser than the boys I had met at the Oberoi Hotel. This is what I made of it:

> Four hundred yards from an army bunker one of the most wanted men in India sips cola and takes the sun in a secluded rose garden. Rafiq Ahmed Dar admits, with evident satisfaction, to killing many Indian soldiers and paramilitary troops. We talk for an hour before bodyguards carrying Kalashnikovs hiss a warning that an army patrol is coming our way. He prepares to fight or flee, but the patrol passes

by. Militants such as Mr Dar are able to dodge tens of thousands of security forces because almost every Kashmiri Muslim supports secession from India, so there are ample places to hide. 'There are precedents for victory over huge armies,' he says. 'The Russians killed hundreds of thousands in Afghanistan but the Afghans won. The Vietnamese defeated the United States. The Iranian revolution succeeded. We, too, will win.

I would bet that Rafiq Ahmed Dar didn't last another year, and his prediction of victory was certainly awry. The life of a militant was short. The security forces introduced an ingenious idea: put masks on captured militants to protect their identities and take them all over Kashmir to point out fellow subversives. Their reward for this betrayal was to be spared torture. They were called 'cats' because only their eyes showed through the masks at night.

There were frequent gunfights between militants and the security forces, especially in Srinagar, and after one of these short-lived street battles a senior military officer proudly showed me the outcome. Lined up on the ground, under a big tarpaulin, were a dozen dead young men. 'Militants,' he said, and flung back the cover to let me see. It was ghastly: a row of brave, ignorant fools, mangled by bullets, their lives uselessly wasted.

I heard about a village that had been plundered by one of the paramilitary groups that kept Kashmir in perpetual terror, and tried to get to it, but it was winter and two attempts to get there were thwarted by snow. My interpreter and I finally got there by walking the last three or four miles when our car could go no further, and it was a terrible sight. All the men and children had been ordered into a building while every woman was raped, including one who was very old. She sat on a rickety wooden chair in the corner of her hut, whining non-stop, psychologically destroyed.

I visited a torture victim in hospital in Srinagar and the doctors told me in grim detail what had been done to him with a sharp pole. The terror in his hollowed-out face, his eyes bulging out of it, was chilling. He placed his hand on mine, perhaps believing this foreigner might somehow have the means to save him. I watched him die, surrounded by family who insisted that he had never been involved in the secessionist movement. Young men were in constant danger of being picked up randomly off the streets and taken to an interrogation centre on the whim of a passing army patrol. Innocence was no defence. Hundreds fled across the border to Pakistan, where they lived in a vast camp enclosed by a tall wire fence, bored and penniless, desperate for news of home, isolated by language and with no future but this.

I spent half a day with them once, listening to their heartbreaking stories and trying not to answer their questions about what was happening back home. They all wanted to know, ridiculously, when Kashmir would be free so they could return. Their heads had been turned by Pakistani propaganda and they believed the grotesque lies fed to them. I couldn't bear to tell them the truth of when they might go home, which was, quite simply, never.

There is a compelling, forbidden place in Kashmir where very few people go and almost nobody is allowed to live. It is hidden behind great mountains that form one side of the Kashmir Valley, within a vast expanse of staggering beauty in the shadow of the Himalayas. It is dangerous there. A mostly unmarked boundary divides it, and it is all but impossible to know where it runs: perhaps this side of a particular tree or that side of a certain ditch, down the middle of a rushing stream or zigzagging over a hill-top. Cross it if you dare. On one side there is India, on the other, Pakistan. This is the India-Pakistan border as it runs through Kashmir and it is officially called the Line of Actual Control. Enemy soldiers stationed on either side of it shoot at each when they feel like it, if only for something to do. Sometimes they blast each other with artillery. Three times since 1947 they have had a proper border war. I obtained permission to visit the Indian front-line to have a close-up look at this interminable unseen conflict, and I mean *very* close.

The journey began from an army base in the mountains. I climbed into a huge armoured vehicle that did three miles to a gallon and roared like a dragon. This beast wound for many miles up a twisting track towards the border, and in one place it passed within range of Pakistani artillery. We traversed this vulnerable stretch at Muslim prayer time in the hope that the gunners would be absent. The vehicle made enough racket to be heard miles away so our presence was hardly a secret, but nobody opened fire. I was being escorted by an officer named Major Santosh Karup, a swashbuckling type who told me as we approached this dangerous stretch,

'We'll drive like hell. There's not much chance of a hit if we keep moving. The danger comes if the driver panics and stops. That's happened before.'

We drove to an altitude of 6,600 feet and walked the last couple of miles along an old goat track to the Line of Control. I was led to a sandbagged bunker from where I looked through a periscope towards Pakistani bunkers nearby. I could see their periscopes looking back at mine. All around there were craters and smashed trees from artillery exchanges. Only two months earlier there had been a firefight for no particular reason, during which both sides fired an estimated 10,000 artillery shells. 'Six of our men were killed and 23 injured,' a brigadier told me. But usually this was a lazy conflict with long silences that might last for weeks followed by flurries of inconsequential violence to break the boredom: not unlike a First World War stalemate, except it had been going on for half a century. In all that time not one inch of territory has been gained by either side. Men fight and die up there because politicians say they must: but it makes not a scrap of sense.

Later, over drinks back at the army base, an officer told me a story about his time stationed in the town of Sopore. Somebody had thrown a hand grenade at a patrol of soldiers but it missed and killed some schoolchildren. This officer suspected the culprit was a local shopkeeper.

'I invited him for a drink. Being a Muslim he was teetotal, but I forced it on him. He quickly got drunk and admitted he'd done it. He said militants had ordered him to throw the grenade or his wife and children would be shot. He told me he was ashamed and wouldn't do it again and I told him he was right, he would never do it again. I took him outside into the trees and shot him three times in the chest with my handgun. Do you know, he was still alive, so I shot him again. I couldn't believe it but he was *still* alive, so I shot him in the head. That finished him.'

'Couldn't you have arrested him and put him on trial?' I asked.

'You'd never get any witnesses to come forward,' he insisted. 'You can't judge what happens here by normal standards. I'd do it again.'

Here was a moral conundrum. The rights of several dead children and the rights of their killer were irreconcilable: justice was carried out unjustly, the law was enforced unlawfully, and what was wrong was at a certain level right. The soldier who summarily shot the shopkeeper, on no authority but his own, was a thoroughly pleasant Hindu family man who talked about missing his wife and children and feeling lonely in Kashmir. What he did was an anomaly to who he was, something he could once never have imagined doing.

This is part of my story describing that trip to the Line of Control:

> Pakistan is in rifle range of India from the Chaukas army post – a collection of steel reinforced bunkers and sandbag placements, artillery, heavy machine-guns and several dozen soldiers, all perched on a Himalayan hill that will soon be pounded by winter blizzards. The mountain passes will close and the

world's most dangerous frontier will hibernate. It is a worn-out war with the air of a boxing tournament between two tired combatants. The soldiers who guard this terrain conduct an old, lazy battle that has flared and faded since 1947. There is silence save for the Jhelum River rushing down the mountains towards Pakistan, cutting through some of the most spectacular terrain on Earth. The border is impossible to seal. It follows no logical geographical path and there is nothing to show where it lies. This is where Pakistani and Indian forces have faced each other since the 1947 war that divided Kashmir.

In one section of the Line of Control there was an old sealed-off bridge crossing a gorge, with Pakistan at one end and India 300 yards away at the other. I wandered around the Pakistan side on a Friday afternoon to witness an old ritual that might fit into a story some time. Pakistani Shia tribesmen regularly went there to shoot at Indian troops, who would respond in kind – harmless fun for those inclined that way. Casualties were zero because everybody was out of rifle range. It always took place after Friday prayers when there was nothing better to do.

But this time something different happened. Instead of rifles the Indians replied with heavy-duty firepower that had everybody diving for cover. The earth around us exploded. I cowered behind some rocks. This barrage lasted for a short while then abruptly stopped, but a young twerp standing next to me behind some rocks decided to fire off a couple

of shots from his handgun. The returning barrage was fero-
cious. Bits of rock were flying around, munitions were biting
into trees and upending the earth. When at last it subsided I
rushed for the perceived safety of a nearby stone hut used by
shepherds in bad weather. It was dark inside and I stumbled
headlong onto my face. I found myself lying amid seven or
eight dead men who had been torn to pieces by high-velocity
armaments that went clean through the walls.

There was yet another warfront beyond Kashmir, out
of sight on top of the world in a place called the Siachen
Glacier in the Himalayas. Nobody lived there, nobody ever
could and nobody ever would. Not a tree, not a weed, not
a single breath of life could exist. It had no strategic or
economic value, it was useless in all practical senses, but
India and Pakistan fought over it. That's what they did. It
was a measure of their pathology.

There were many ways that soldiers died up there. If
they stayed too long their lungs filled with water, or they
might fall through snow-covered holes. They could slide
off hidden ledges. Avalanches got them, and there was the
constant danger of going blind. Lots did. I saw some of them
from the Indian side, eyes bandaged, in the military hospital
in the small town of Leh, in Ladakh, a supply centre for
hauling men and equipment by helicopter to Siachen. This
was a fiercely expensive war for India, forced as it was to
rely on helicopters to deliver every item of supplies. When
the weather turned bad the men on the mountain were
entirely alone. Pakistan, however, could reach its side of

Siachen with vehicles and, on the highest stretches, mules.

This was a war that could not be fought. Artillery was useless because a shell pretty much went where it liked in the thin air. Soldiers went on patrol weighed down by clothing and oxygen tanks and couldn't have fought a mouse. The highest war in the world was expensive and absurd.

The Pakistani side allowed me to visit. I was taken in a Lynx helicopter, which had been stripped of all possible weight to give it maximum height, and we headed to the main base at around 10,000 feet. The pilot asked me casually if I smoked or had a heart condition, because if I did I might die. I suggested that he should have asked me this before we left, and he laughed. When we landed and I stepped out into the snow the world started to wobble. Tea and a brief rest balanced me.

The brigadier heading Pakistan's Siachen Brigade described the challenges of this terrain but wouldn't be drawn into discussing the pointlessness of it. He took me all over the base and then we had a fine lunch. As I climbed back into the helicopter he told the pilot to take me on a tour of the mountains, and it turned into a wild ride. Wind and thermals punched us left and right and up and down as we flew around those impossibly spectacular mountains, which seemed disturbingly close at times but the pilot assured me that was an optical illusion. 'Take a left there!' I would shout. 'Take us over that peak.' It was the trip of a lifetime. The weather suddenly turned nasty, as it does in a heartbeat up there, and we fled down to earth chased by an angry storm.

At home with Timmy the cat.

A fresh-faced 23-year-old in my Kimberly days

Even fresher-faced – a trainee reporter on the
Thurrock Gazette in Grays, Essex.

No potatoes or cabbages then? Mujahidin warlords announced a ban on poppy cultivation and a return to conventional agriculture – a lie as big as the poppy fields being tended by this farmer deep inside Kandahar province. Within a few days those fat near-ripe poppies would be sliced open and the milky contents sent off to be converted into heroin.

Taking aim at distant rocks in the Khyber Pass with a borrowed Kalashnikov.

Guns going cheap. Tribesmen in the North West Frontier Province (as it was then known) have for generations made top-quality weapons. All buyers welcome, cash only, no questions asked.

Indian friends always said Valerie was one of the very few foreigners who could carry off Indian clothes.

Performing a puja (religious ceremony) with a Hindu priest to rid the Foreign Correspondents' Club in Delhi of its resident alcoholic ghost. Flanking me are John Rettie of *The Guardian*, Tim McGirk of *The Independent*, an Indian journalist, Jan McGirk of the *Daily Express*, and John Anderson of the *Washington Post*.

Around every corner in India there is a surprise and a welcome. This puppeteer happened to drop into a dhaba (a roadside kitchen) where I was drinking tea in a remote village in southern India, and he invited me to practise his art.

In my element – the *Times* office in Delhi, which was a converted bedroom in my house. The house is now a yoga centre.

In the Oval Office of the White House with President Reagan, who was absolutely charming.

With King Wangchuck of Bhutan at his palace in Thimpu, the capital, where his four wives lived together with lots of children. The king chose to live alone in a wooden house in the hills – "if you had four wives, wouldn't you?"

I furtively removed this propaganda poster from a wall in Buenos Aires during the Falklands War - or the Malvinas War, as Argentina knows it. It reads: "We have already demonstrated our peaceful vocation. Now we will demonstrate our fighting spirit. Two virtues are equally true for Argentinians. Both with rich historical antecedents. We know how to give life for our Malvinas. And we know how to give death to anybody who seeks to seize them."

A mock-up of a front page of *The Times* presented to me by fellow journalists before I left India (and *The Times*) and headed for Spain. Every "story" was a barracking send-up of me, each one throughly deserved. It is one of my most treasured possessions.

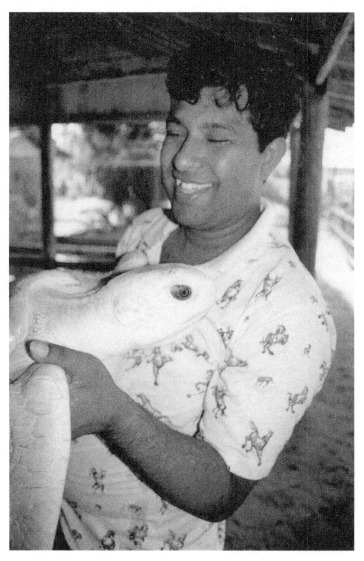

Rosie the albino turtle nuzzles her best friend, who raised her from birth and protected her from attack by other turtles confounded by her colour.

THE TIMES

1 Pennington Street, London E1 9XN
Telephone: 01-782 5000   Telex: 262141

FOR THE ATTENTION OF CHRIS THOMAS

FROM THE TIMES, FOREIGN, LONDON

FAX NO. 010 1 202 371 0686

DATE : 14th May 1989

****

.Thomas has packed the Suntan oil.
His topee's new and shiny,
For soon his blood will start to boil
(and also taste quite briny).

He's off to pastures new and hot
Where the noonday sun is cruel.
He'll find a tot costs quite a lot
- though he may well save on fuel.

He'll cultivate (shades of the Raj)
The British sahib's ways;
No doubt he'll occupy a barge
on Kashmir holidays.

He'll lead his servants quite a dance
in his own palatial haven
and foster an imperious stance
(It's a pity he's clean shaven).

We wish him well and hope to see
his bylines - well I'm blessed !
He's changed his name to Bannerjee,
by India quite obsessed !

****

The best of luck, keep in touch...

Registered Office: Times Newspapers Limited, P.O. Box 495, Virginia Street, London E1 9XY
Registered No. 894646 England

This, too, is treasured by me. It was written by a bard on *The Times*
Foreign Desk and faxed to me in the Delhi office the day I arrived to
take up my assignment.

The three incomparable M's – Maria, Matthew and Melanie.

CHAPTER TEN

Pakistan commands superlatives. Failed state, pit of human misery, a dystopia – for starters. It is run by shamelessly corrupt politicians (with a few noble exceptions) who operate in the shadow of an ambitious military that seizes power when it thinks it can. Feudal landlords enjoy a staggering, primordial privilege. Its religious order dominates and rules the lives of those who adhere to it as well as those who don't. It is riven by tribal, ethnic, linguistic and religious divisions and, of course, it is massively poor apart from the creamy layer who flaunt their privilege. Only international charity keeps the country afloat, because it is bankrupt. It was bankrupt the day it was born. Naturally I went there constantly.

But first I had to solicit an entry visa from a congenial fellow called Mufti at the Pakistan High Commission in Delhi, who would chat cheerfully while pouring tea into china cups as we awaited the stamp in my passport from functionaries working in mysterious isolation upstairs. I knew Mufti for years, but he never leaked anything that didn't go into a teacup. I would probe away and he would pour more tea and smile enigmatically. Usually he granted only single-entry visas, but with a little artwork I sometimes turned '1' into '4' in those less technological times.

Getting to Islamabad, the capital, usually meant flying from Delhi to Lahore, then enduring a taxi drive for several hours on one of the world's most lethal highways. Another option was to head north to India's Punjab and take the only legal land crossing at a place called Wagah. This would entail some enthusiastic searching of bags on the Pakistani side for concealed booze. A bottle of Johnnie Walker Black goes a long way in Pakistan – not for me because I don't like the stuff much, but plenty of people in Pakistan do. Sometimes a kindly border official would wink and let me keep it.

The Wagah crossing presented a poignant reminder that this had been one country before the creation of Pakistan in 1947. Indian porters carried your bags along a short no-man's-land stretch of road and deposited them on a white line – the official border. Pakistani porters in Islamic green picked them up and shared a greeting with their Indian counterparts in their shared language, Punjabi. They could well be distantly related, but officially they were adversaries.

At dusk each side tried to out-do the other in a theatrical ceremony of foot-stomping, trumpet blasting, goose-stepping and snappy about-turns. The gates were then ceremonially closed and locked, the flags lowered, and the two countries became symbolically sealed off for the night. But it always seemed an unnatural separation whenever I crossed that way: every village could belong to either side, the food was the same, the people were the same (religion aside). The anchor-stones of 5,000 years of shared language, history and culture yielded little to the feeble tugs of this artificial politicians' division.

There was one person in Pakistan who rose above everybody else, and, like Sister Anna in Ulster, he cared not a damn for publicity, otherwise he would assuredly have been nominated for the Nobel Peace Prize. It's a disgrace that it never happened. His name was Abdul Sattar Edhi. He has been called the Mother Teresa of Pakistan, which is not fair because he was nothing like her. For a start, none of his charity's funds ended up in Rome or bank accounts in New York. He was always on the move, improving and saving lives. I once travelled half the country trying to catch up with him but never did.

If I couldn't find the man, I could at least find his work. Down a back street in Karachi I entered a decrepit building through a door that was never locked, and at the top of concrete steps on the dimly lit landing was a little metal cot with fluffy blankets in it. Every day babies were placed there by mothers too poor to care for them, before slipping away unseen. All that was asked of them was to leave some indication of the child's religion.

This centre and its solitary secret cot was one of 350

of its kind across Pakistan, all run by Edhi. He sought adoptive parents for all the children left in his care but if necessary he would look after them in his own orphanages. Thousands upon thousands of children passed through his centres; he was the conscience of the country. He ran the world's largest fleet of private ambulances and never took a rupee of public money, relying instead on private donations. He voiced contempt for politicians and didn't want them or their money anywhere near him, aware that they would always exact a price.

Apart from my fixation with Edhi, everything I wrote about Pakistan tended to be about grim stuff. I attended a madrassa (Islamic school) for a day in the tribal heartland of Peshawar and watched classes of children repeating words read to them from the Koran by groups of mullahs. This would go on for hour after mind-bending hour, day after day, year after year, relentlessly pummelling the children's brains with the mullahs' inerrant, twisted versions of Islam. After a decade of this the kids would leave school functionally illiterate but able to recite great swathes of the Koran by heart.

I nearly got my comeuppance in Lahore when covering the trial of a 14-year-old Christian boy accused of blaspheming the Prophet. The charges were cooked up by mullahs as part of their ceaseless campaign against Christians and minority Muslim sects. I wrote two versions of that story, one saying the boy had been convicted and would be put to death, the other that he had been found not guilty and released. This was because the verdict was due shortly before deadline and the paper needed a pre-written story to throw into the front page.

As soon as the verdict was announced – not guilty – I ran from the courthouse for the nearest telephone to tell the paper which version to use. A hostile crowd, baying in outrage outside the courthouse when the verdict became known, decided I was running away – from what, or why, I had no idea, any more than they did. They wanted somebody to pay for the verdict, and this foreigner was as good as any.

There were perhaps 30 of them and they caught me. I was being kicked and punched and thought that was my lot. I was on the ground when one of the lawyers in the trial, still wearing formal garb, burst through and used his authority and loud voice to restrain the crowd. 'Do you want to be hanged for murder?' he shouted at them. 'I recognise some of you. I'll make sure you hang.' He slowly inched backwards out of the throng, taking me with him, his arm around my shoulder. 'Keep walking, don't stop, look to the ground,' he whispered. He talked constantly to the crowd in both English and Urdu. He got me into his car and pulled slowly away, the mob yelling and banging on it. He probably saved my life. And I caught the deadline.

Next day I tracked him down on the phone to thank him. He told me never to contact him again and hung up. I can only assume he was facing death threats for saving me. As for the acquitted boy, whose name was Salamat Masih, his life was over, despite his acquittal. I don't know what became of him but he would have been a target for the rest of his life, which I suspect was very short, given the nature of things in Pakistan. The country's motto is Faith, Unity, Discipline – omitting, rather significantly, any mention of Freedom.

The marriage of the British heiress Jemima Goldsmith to the Pakistani cricketing legend Imran Khan was a news sensation. She converted to Islam, set about learning Urdu, and insanely agreed to live with her husband in Pakistan. Before she moved there I let rip with an article in which I tried to give a flavour of the country she would inhabit. The headline was 'The Fate That Awaits Jemima'.

Some excerpts:

> The shackles of a strict Islamic society will click invisibly but firmly shut the moment she steps out of the Very Very Important Persons (VVIP) section of Lahore airport into the thick heat of the Punjabi summer.
>
> There are only two classes of women in Pakistan: upper and lower. The upper are distinguished by their use of English. Some are newspaper editors, ambassadors, senior civil servants, doctors and lawyers. Even they have to toe the line.
>
> If Jemima goes to a restaurant in the exclusive Gulmarg district of Lahore there will be no wine on the menu because it is illegal, although some restaurants will serve illicit liquor in teapots. If she fancies

a tipple at home she will have to get to know the neighbourhood bootlegger.

She says she plans to work at a newspaper in Lahore. If it happens to be at the office of Dawn she will have to negotiate the traffic turmoil on the Mall then find a little door with peeling paint, beyond which lies a stinking staircase that rises into a clutch of offices covered in grime. The atmosphere is one of penury and unremitting boredom.

The nightlife Jemima enjoys in London does not exist in Pakistan: no clubs or bars, no theatres she would care to visit, no culture she could understand. In her spare time she might decide to explore the life-styles of lower-class women. She would soon find a pile of reports from Amnesty International and other human rights organisations portraying a country that could be from the Dark Ages.

Women are jailed for being raped, and once behind bars they stand a chance of being raped again. Under Muslim rape law a woman must provide four male Muslim eyewitnesses to prove there was penetration: the testimony of women carries no legal weight.

Jemima will hear a lot about the Hudood Ordinances, or Islamic penal laws, which criminalise adultery. Punishments include stoning to death and public flogging. A woman who complains to police that she was raped runs the risk of being prosecuted for adultery. She will find that Christians are mostly at the bottom of the social heap and that Jews are hated, which could be a problem given that Sir James

Goldsmith, her father, is half Jewish and a good friend of Israel.

After four years Jemima fled the country to avoid imprisonment on cooked-up charges of exporting antique tiles. She returned fretfully when the charges were dropped, but after a few more years she left for good and got divorced. How she lasted so long I don't know.

There is an off-limits area in the tribal territories of north-western Pakistan where Afridi tribesmen make guns – machine guns, semi-automatic rifles, shotguns, hunting rifles, hand guns, little close-range assassination pistols (accurate to three feet), and even (they claim) artillery pieces by special order. Their specialist weapon is a Kalashnikov look-alike. This industry is conducted in and around a dusty town called Darra Adam Khel in what used to be called the North West Frontier Province, near the Khyber Pass. Outsiders are supposed to get permits to go there, but they are rarely granted so I went illegally in a bashed-up taxi that drew no attention.

Darra boasted scores of well-stocked gun shops in its main street, sitting incongruously among fruit-and-vegetable shops, clothing stores, pharmacies and shoe sellers. Nobody raised an eyebrow at the rat-a-tat of shooting as gunmakers demonstrated their wares to would-be buyers on open ground behind their shops. I watched a woman buying vegetables from a market stall while a man next to her fired a Kalashnikov into the air. She didn't give him a second glance.

Making weapons has been an industry in Darra for generations, mostly conducted in small family-run workshops and people's houses. Children polish the butts, dad works the lathes, mum fetches and carries, and nobody asks nor cares where the guns end up. The iron for these weapons sometimes came from the wheels of old trains, because the quality was good.

I asked a shop owner if he had ever delivered weapons to the Indian side of Kashmir for the separatist fighters there. Of course, he said, often. There were plenty of ways across and indeed some people he knew crossed over all the time because they had a wife on both sides. How soon could he fulfil an order for, say, 50 Kalashnikovs? 'Tomorrow,' he ventured. He seemed perfectly serious.

On one of his shelves there was a row of what looked like fountain pens. 'Why are you selling these?' I asked. He smiled and took one down. Removing the top revealed a tiny barrel, and a plunger at the other end was the trigger. The bullet was tiny. This gun, he informed me matter-of-factly, was for killing somebody close-up in a crowd. I inquired where somebody would get ammunition for such a specialist item. 'Here,' he said. 'We make bullets for everything we sell.'

I asked to try a Kalashnikov – he insisted his were better than the real thing – and bought 20 rounds. We went out the back of the shop and I fired at a far-distant rock. Bullseye. And another and another. It was impossible to miss. I turned to say something to him and touched the hair trigger, releasing a round that ricocheted off the stony ground. He yelled and snatched the gun away angrily.

Darra was also a player in the drugs trade, but its activities didn't come close to what went on beyond it. In the desert state of Baluchistan I watched scores of armed men, Afghans by the look of them, escorting a convoy of drug-laden lorries along the Pakistan-Afghan frontier, untroubled by any official intervention. I wasn't privy to some big secret here: everybody knew about these regular shipments because local people were closely involved with them. I wrote:

> They kick up enough dust to be seen 20 miles away but nobody intercepts them. The Pakistan frontier police, with barely enough funds to buy bullets, look on impotently. Here, the battle against drugs has been lost. Much of the consignment is on the way to Britain. The caravan includes a portable laboratory for converting opium into heroin. On the Pakistan coast men are waiting in wooden dhows to carry the contraband to mother ships waiting over the horizon.

Peshawar, capital of north-western Pakistan, hosted conmen, militia bosses, religious fanatics, tribal chiefs, dirty politicians, corrupt army officers, drug traffickers, smugglers, terrorists and hit-men. Its intrigues lent an aura of frontier-town menace. This was the starting point for the journey through the Khyber Pass into Afghanistan.

Getting a permit to enter the Khyber was a bureaucratic

rigmarole. It required spending half a day in grubby offices adorned with decades-old piles of paperwork flapping in the blast of ceiling fans. Within this crumbling detritus a stern-faced bureaucrat would sit at his desk pondering your documentation for an unnecessarily long time, puffed full with the authority of his position, before reaching for the all-important rubber stamp and slapping it down hard enough to reach all four carbon copies, then passing it on to another bureaucrat down the line. 'Next,' he would shout to the waiting queues after removing the top copy and handing the rest to an obsequious underling standing at his elbow. This man would shuffle off to deliver the remaining copies to other *babus* awaiting their moments of glory with the rubber stamp.

Each of these gloomy-faced men had a tiny and precise duty to perform. This dividing of jobs into halves and quarters was a way of providing pitifully-paid work to armies of people who would otherwise be unemployed. As in India, working for a government bureaucracy was always cherished because it provided security and status – and opportunities for *baksheesh*.

With the paperwork finally completed, you were escorted to an open-backed government truck and off you went through the rugged byways of Peshawar and on to the Khyber and finally to the border with Afghanistan, accompanied all the way by an armed guard too old to be more than an ornament. For a little money he would loan you his Kalashnikov and take pictures of you aiming it at the mountains, and sometimes let you fire off a round if his weapon happened to have a bullet in it. But that was an extra.

The Khyber has power. It carries energy and mystique from centuries of violent history, and it isn't hard to imagine Genghis Kahn thundering through. The road twists and turns in a series of hairpin bends, cutting through sinister, silent, near-dead mountains. Here and there rocks on the roadside are painted with British regimental insignia from far-flung times, faded but still clear. They seemed unofficial tombstones for British soldiers defeated in three Anglo-Afghan wars, left intact through the generations because Afghans respect the British as warriors – unlike the contempt they feel for the Russians, who foolishly invaded the country and were soundly thrashed. Afghan fighters have a couple of secret weapons: they don't fear dying and they endure a climate that kills others. They have never lost a war. Be it 42 degrees or minus five, they endure.

I went through the Khyber many times and never lost the thrill of it. Getting to Kabul took five, seven or ten hours on a decrepit road that was dirt most of the way, depending on who and what was encountered. I did it once with my friend Molly Moore of *The Washington Post* in the back of a pick-up truck that bounced around like a rodeo horse. We wanted to get to Kabul to report on the latest war there, and were stopped repeatedly by armed gangs wanting cigarettes. We had wisely brought several cartons.

These unpredictable, illiterate mountain-men had spent their lives killing people – either Russians or fellow Afghans. There were boys of five and six packing pistols. Men who had never seen a white woman, and with an uncovered face to boot, stared hard at Molly and there were uncomfortable moments. Molly, a veteran of hot-headed places, handled the situation coolly. An American Pashtu-speaking journalist I travelled with on one of these journeys – an Associated Press guy – had a Kalashnikov aimed at his guts by a youth who didn't like being answered back, and he would have died but for the last-second shouted intervention of a white-bearded elder. Death was no big deal to them.

Tank and artillery fire were intense as Molly and I neared Kabul, and at dusk we took refuge in the mosquito-infested basement of a bombed-out building. We had brought two vital products: torches and mosquito spray, and without either we would have been in crisis. The night was noisy with war, and one enormous explosion took out nearly all the broken windows above us in a riot of smashing glass. A tank had stationed itself nearby and was shooting one shell after another, which drew a heavy reply.

At dawn the tank had gone, but we nevertheless agreed it would be madness to proceed and decided to return to Jalalabad, close to the border with Pakistan. This was a poignant journey, because the same road had been taken by the only survivor of the first Anglo-Afghan war, who reached Jalalabad on a starving horse that dropped dead the next day. This man was the regimental surgeon, and had been allowed to live to tell the story. His name was William Brydon. All the other 4,500 British soldiers were shot by snipers or left to starve on the streets of Kabul. The British commander of that ill-fated mission was said to have boasted to Afghan tribal leaders when he entered Kabul that not a single shot had been fired to oppose them. The response was, 'It is true that you entered our country unopposed. But how will you get out?'

The Afghan ambassador in Delhi, who I visited occasionally for background, gave me a tip: go to Kabul immediately. He wouldn't say why. He issued me with a visa and a few days later I headed to Kabul on one of the last few clattering aircraft operated by Ariana Airlines, the national carrier, whose name reflects the Afghans' belief that they are of Aryan stock. It looked and sounded overdue for the knacker's yard.

Landing in Kabul was always a touch wild, and pilots loved it because it involved real flying. The objective was to avoid missiles. This entailed coming in fast and high before dropping quickly to low altitude, then twisting and turning through the mountains before banking hard and skimming low across the ground towards the runway.

I checked into what was left of the Inter-Continental Hotel, part of which was bombed-out rubble. Running water was sporadic, electricity was mostly off, I was the only guest and there was nothing to eat but eggs. I went out for street food but nowhere was open. Back to the hotel for an omelette.

In the morning, still wondering why I was there, I went for a look round. The streets were silent. None of the usual gunmen were to be seen, there were no pick-up trucks tearing around with fighters in the back, no hawkers, no beggars, no traffic, and still nowhere to eat. Even the markets hadn't opened. The city had died. Not only did I have a hotel to myself: I had the town, too. Overnight, unannounced and unheard (at least by me), the militia that controlled Kabul had moved out. This meant that a more powerful force was on the way. Whose? Which warlord? Worse than the last? I had lately acquired a piece of technology called a satellite telex, about the size of a shoe-box, which enabled me to file from any remote area from a laptop computer so long as there was a power source. The hotel found a small generator and I was able to send copy to London.

That night it happened. Tracer bullets filled the night sky like festive fireworks, emanating from several places outside the city. This was an announcement that the new ruler was coming. Next day tanks rolled into the streets and took up positions. I was in the hotel lobby as armed men burst through the doors. They ran around yelling but quickly calmed down and began gambolling on the lobby sofas and armchairs: their first experience of soft seats. They were laughing like kids in a playground. In the brief interludes when the electricity came on they went up and down in the lifts, agog at such technology. When they found the bar they smashed it up.

The new ruler was a Tajik called General Mohammad Massoud. By Afghan standards he was a moderate and Kabul returned fitfully to life, but not for long. Other warlords – Pashtuns – soon launched a siege to drive him out, killing 50,000 people over the coming years and reducing most of the city to rubble. Different parts of the city fell to different factions, and crossing from one side to the other could be an ordeal. This is how I described it:

> There is a different government on every street
> corner. Here it is Uzbek militia, there it is Tajik
> Mujahidin. Somewhere else Shia Muslims or the
> long-persecuted Hazaras flexing their muscles. The
> pattern of control changes constantly, turning a
> simple journey into a gamble. The battle-lines of this
> new war, coming four months after the end of the
> last one, is essentially Pashtun versus non-Pashtun.
> It has been thus for centuries.

Vast refugee camps appeared in distant locations, and I used to visit them with great reluctance. There is nothing sadder, nothing more awful, than five or ten thouand homeless and hopeless people packed together in a sea of tents, raggedly dressed, bored, frightened, displaced, dirty and broken. I went back time and again to Kabul during this terrible siege and witnessed the city being bombed to dust. One time I went wandering around an old Mogul tomb for a short diversion and froze to the spot when I saw a signpost a few yards away bearing a skull and crossbones and a notice declaring that this was an uncleared minefield. I tiptoed back across my tracks as best I could remember them.

Afghans are an unfathomable paradox. I frequently sat cross-legged on the floor with different warlords eating lunch or dinner and watching the friendly banter of their top men. The culture of hospitality to strangers runs deep, and invitations to sit and eat were given out freely. One memorable meal was taken with a large group of Mujahidin tribesmen who had been busy fighting and killing all morning with some enemy over the hill, and with the meal over they clambered back into their war machines and roared back to the fight as naturally as if returning to the office. Some were young enough to have known nothing but war, and this life was perfectly natural to them. They could not have been more welcoming or generous to this stranger, and they shouted and waved their rifles in a cheery goodbye as they roared off to war.

I was in Afghanistan in 1992 soon after the Russian-backed government collapsed and a Pashtun militia – the Mujahidin – seized control. The leader of the ousted government was a Russian-sponsored puppet called President Mohammed Najibullah, a tall and powerfully built former head of the secret service with a reputation for brutality. He tried to flee to India as his government collapsed but left it just a few hours too late. His plane was on the runway ready to go, but he was turned away and forced to return to Kabul, where he took refuge in a United Nations compound and remained there for the next four years. After that an even more fanatical Pashtun militia, the Taleban, seized control of the city and dragged Najibullah off to be tortured and murdered. I saw him hanging by the neck from a lamp post in the street. He had been castrated, judging by what I could see of him, and there he remained for many days.

I spent some time piecing together his final hours and it boiled down to this: he was so big there was no way of disguising or hiding him. He couldn't be dressed in a burka or as a peasant and smuggled out. His size was the death of him. His wife and children had been living in Delhi for the previous four years and almost every day he called them on a satellite phone. He would have known the fate that was coming for him and would have had time to say goodbye. What a terrible conversation that must have been.

There were no banks in war-shattered Kabul. There was nothing much at all save for a row of tacky shops known bizarrely as Chicken Street, where it was possible to buy canned products, fruit and vegetables, and maybe if you were lucky a tube of toothpaste or a bar of soap, not to mention under-the-counter booze from time to time. If you needed money the only source was the Money Market, consisting of a dozen or so little shops located next to a river-cum-sewer that chugged by in a foul yellow slop.

The shop owners were mostly Afghan-born Sikhs. It worked thus: you asked for a thousand pounds' worth of Afghanis, the local currency. They gave you a half a sackful of them and you handed over a personal cheque – in my case drawn on my Barclays account in England. This could take six months to clear, but it always did. The Sikhs claimed the system was based on trust, but in fact it was based on menace. Nobody who bounced a cheque was beyond the reach of the worldwide Afghan diaspora.

> Jawad, 13, stands on a chair in the middle of one of
> Kabul's main roads balancing a chunk of waste metal
> on his shoulders. His legs are shaking. He has been
> there for hours. Hundreds of people stare silently at

this new version of the stocks. Children chant 'thief.' This was medieval Afghanistan yesterday.

Kabul, always Afghan's most liberal bastion, hates the fanatical Taleban rulers. Jawad had taken a few pieces of scrap metal in a town that is a scrapyard from 17 years of war. A youth a few years older, apparently mute, stood on a chair beside him, holding a battered drawer from a filing cabinet. When anybody spoke to him he replied with a gagging sound. People seemed as disgusted by the abuse as they were fascinated by it. The rest of the stolen goods lay between the boys: bits of a bicycle, a holed bucket, twisted metal from a car.

I witnessed this incident by chance. A mullah, illiterate as most are, had ordered the punishment and was pleased by the attention of the crowds. He flashed a great big smile and shook my hand enthusiastically when I approached, told me the boys' names and indicated with chopping motions what would happen next time they stole. He was in ebullient mood as he flashed triumphant little looks towards the boys he was torturing. There is no way to rationalise the contradictions of a convivial brute.

This was a snapshot of life under the Taleban, which had swept aside a patchwork of tribal warlords and replaced them with an ultra-orthodox Islamic order. It banned girls going to school, banned all non-religious music, ordered men to grow beards and attend mosque five times a day, banned women from teaching and attending university.

Women had to be accompanied outside the home by a male relative and wear a full-length burka with a mesh covering the face, which impeded breathing and shut off peripheral vision.

I bought an Afghan burka from a Kabul marketplace once and took it home to Delhi to show people what monstrous things they were. Val tried it on and instantly tore it off. Not only was it hard to breathe inside it, but the 'head' was small and clung tightly, like a clamp.

Banning women from working was a catastrophe for thousands of war widows. The consequences were evident when I visited Kabul Orphanage, which was bursting with children abandoned by war widows unable to feed them. It housed 800 children and more were left at the door every day. No women were allowed to tend them because that constituted work, and some elderly men, working without pay, were doing their woeful best. For breakfast the children had tea and plain bread; dinner was peas, beans and rice. One lone woman risked her life by turning up every day to help.

The windows had no glass in them, there were no toys or games, there was no heating. Electricity and water supplies were erratic. The kitchen was a soot-blackened dungeon in which the cook stirred food with a shovel in giant cauldrons over wood fires, the smoke escaping through a hole in the roof. The children sat on benches at ranks of tables, skinny, timid and quiet. Most looked sick, but there was no medical attention.

The lone woman arrived before dawn unless delayed

by Taleban patrols, threw her burka aside and set to work until it was dark again. The men, also risking punishment, conspired with her. If Taleban soldiers turned up, they would rush around hiding her. My article about this courageous woman – unnamed, of course – prompted a call on a Reuters satellite phone from Sarah Ferguson, the Duchess of York, who wanted to send funds from a charity she was involved with. I had to tell her that sending money was impossible because Afghanistan had no infrastructure to receive it: that it had been bombed into pre-history. I returned to the orphanage months later on my next visit and a little help was trickling through, I think from a United Nations agency, and the woman was still there, as were the men, still working for nothing, still risking their lives. The orphanage by then had 1000 children. Later, the Taleban relented and allowed a small number of women to work there.

The greatest achievement of Afghanistan is that it exists. Most of it looked like Armageddon when last I saw it. Despite constantly waging war with itself, people believed in it and were perversely proud of it, and there was never a hint of any region wanting to break away to form an independent state. Scratch a Pashtun, a Turkmen, a Tajik or an Uzbek and there is an Afghan. It's not like that in Pakistan, where people are Punjabis or Sindhis or Baluch, and don't greatly relate to the country. The attachment of Afghans to their shattered land gives their country its greatest and only strength, and that is why it will never fragment. These were my first impressions of it after travelling through the Khyber

Pass to Kabul:

The tragedy of perhaps the world's poorest nation is evident immediately beyond the Durand Line, an illogical, divisive and hated symbol of imperialism that used to mark the border with British India and today demarks the Pakistan-Afghan frontier. On either side of a narrow and hopelessly congested street there are a couple of stone gateposts but no gate. This is the border.

Beyond it lies the Islamic Emirate of Afghanistan, where the world ends. There is only emptiness save for an occasional band of gaily dressed Gypsies with camels and goats traipsing the hills looking for grass. The road to Kabul, such as it exists, is dotted with hulks of tanks and other military hardware from several permutations of warfare over two decades. They will never rust in the parched air, remaining as permanent monuments.

Children and old men with shovels fill in potholes with dirt and stones – freelance labourers hoping a little money might be tossed to them. One-legged young men on crutches, victims of mines, are the most pathetic of the roadside beggars. To left and right of the road, all the way to Kabul, there are smashed villages: more monuments to wars.

Afghanistan does have history unrelated to war: a history of trade. It was the main crossroads on the trading routes between India and Central Asia, and Kabul Museum had a priceless collection of 100,000 artefacts dating from prehistory to the 20th century. By the mid-1990s it had all gone, every piece destroyed or looted. After a rocket attack destroyed much of the building and its contents the United Nations shifted everything that was left into a fortified basement. A warlord came along one day and blew the metal doors off it, and what survived of the precious contents he piled into trucks and hauled them away to be sold off like gimcracks. Various pieces have turned up around the world at auctions and one was acquired by a corrupt Pakistani politician who boasted that he paid more than £50,000 for it. He said he would return it when there was peace in Afghanistan. He was on safe ground there.

Afghanistan was by this time nothing more than a vast wasteland, ungoverned, war-torn, brutalised, diseased and substantially abandoned, its very history sold off, its soul lost. Most of the villages, where 90 per cent of the massively depleted population lived, were medieval: no sanitary water, no electricity, no medical care, no schools, no transportation, scant food. Natural disasters struck constantly – an endless round of earthquakes, drought, snowstorms and floods. It has one of the hardest climates on earth.

I reached one of the remotest of its beleaguered villages, a place called Kol, by helicopter to report on a massive earthquake in which tens of thousands may have died: the number will never be known. I travelled with a volunteer British doctor and a team of medics whose work was inspiring and humbling. The scale of devastation was clear as we came in to land: it was absolute. Dead and injured were strewn around, no buildings were intact, survivors wandered around in shock, the women wailed frantically.

A man came forward with his six-year-old daughter, who had infected facial wounds and possibly two broken legs. She was shifted to one side as non-priority. A boy was found to have a bone infection unrelated to the quake. 'He'll have to lose that leg,' the doctor said as he looked in vain for somewhere to wash his hands. 'There's a lot of impetigo here. It's extremely infectious.' Some men wouldn't allow their injured wives to be examined, but without an interpreter it was impossible to reason with them.

For an hour or two the doctor – his name was Gilbert Greenall – assessed who might be saved and who must die: a triage of terrible and unavoidable brutality. A few serious cases went back with us on the helicopter to Faizabad, where international relief facilities were being established, but real help wouldn't reach Kol until the next day. By then, many of those laid out on the dust would be dead.

The rulers of Kandahar Province in southern Afghanistan announced a ban on poppy production. Most heroin in the United States and Europe came from Afghanistan, so it was big news. My first reaction was: bullshit.

When it came time for poppy-harvesting I went to Kandahar to see all those fields of potatoes and cabbages that were promised. I hired a truck from a local man, found a good-enough translator, and off we went into the hinterlands. We stopped for green tea and lunch at a roadside shack. It would have been chicken or mutton with a slab of thick dry bread. It always was.

Soon, pink and pretty against the dusty land, we came across fields of poppies swaying in the breeze, their firm heads nearly as big as tennis balls. We approached a farmer in the field, who said he was pleased with the crop. Any day now the heads would be slit in the cool evening air so the sticky milk-white sap could ooze out – the stuff of opium and then heroin. The farmer wouldn't be paid much for his product, but the warlords who controlled the region would see handsome profits. All over the ground there were used American artillery shells, a legacy from the 1980s when the United States provided military aid to help oust the Soviet Union, which had occupied the country. 'America sent us these,' the farmer said, picking up one of the old shells. In the other hand he held a poppy. 'And we're sending them this.'

I sat under a tree writing my story on my laptop computer, then asked the driver to start the truck engine while I attached crocodile clips to the battery and set about filing copy to London from my satellite telex. He would have been no more amazed if I had beamed myself into space.

The BBC World Service quoted the story in their Pashtun service next day. An Afghan United Nations worker rapped on the door of the room where I was staying in a UN compound and told me I should get out immediately because certain people were very angry. He drove me to a small UN plane that was coincidentally in Kandahar and about to leave for Pakistan. I was soon gratefully gone.

Afghanistan's national game – some call it sport – is *buzkashi,* which means 'goat-snatcher.' It's a national metaphor: no rules, no prescribed number of combatants, no clear teams, no absolute winners, no time limits, no fixed boundaries, no referees, no restraints on violence. Violence is the point.

It goes like this: men thunder round an area of rough ground on horses, leaning hard over to seize the headless and hoof-less carcass of a goat or sheep. This is the 'ball.' They could use a real ball, but that would lack gore. Gore is important. The approximate aim is to dump a chunk of carcass into a goal circle, but the carcass gets torn into so many chunks it's impossible to know which is in play – or if any is. The one game I watched, in the northern town of Mazar-i-Sharif, ended when there wasn't enough left of the goat to fight over. Bloody bits lay everywhere, pulverised into the ground. Genghis Khan liked *buzkashi* and introduced a variation using the bodies of enemies. I have heard it said that Afghans did the same with captured Russian soldiers in the 1980s. It may even be true.

Mazar-i-Sharif is where I lost the appetite for covering conflicts. Something clicked inside me and I didn't want to do it again. It wasn't a decision: it felt like an instruction, and there was no arguing with it. All I wanted was to get out of there, but that was the problem. There was no way out.

Mazar, an Uzbek town, was under siege from Pashtun warlords in a wider fight for control of the country. Fighting blocked the way out to the east, west and south, and it was getting closer by the hour. The town was all but defenceless from marauders. North was the only possible way to go, but the bridge across the River Oxus into Uzbekistan was sealed tight and heavily guarded by Uzbek forces.

The hegemon of Mazar was a jackbooted brute called General Dostum, whose name perversely translates from Uzbek into 'my friend.' One account I heard about his tactics was to stake out his enemies and have tanks drive slowly over them, feet first. I met him once in his fortress. He was in army fatigues and possessed an enormous, commanding presence, the kind that lowers the temperature of a room. This was the man the Pashtun invaders were trying to dislodge. The battle was close-range and soon would be street-to-street.

Several foreign journalists, me included, were staying in the same boarding house when armed looters burst in. I was carrying a few thousand dollars, which I flung under a mattress a second before they entered the room. One man tried to seize my laptop computer and I resisted. A Kalashnikov in my belly persuaded me to give it to him. Try as he might, he couldn't open it, having never encountered such a contraption, and in frustration he threw it into the air and walked away. I dived for it, caught it just before it would have smashed on the hard floor, and hurt my shoulder. I thought at first it was broken. They never did check under the mattress, and with my computer I could still file.

Over the following days, fighting reached the edge of town. We retreated to the basement during one particularly heavy bombardment as tanks fired outwards from the streets around us and heavy ordinance came back. Rifle-fire crackled like fireworks. There was a small window high in the wall through which we could see flashes of light. A random bullet, or perhaps a piece of shrapnel, came through it and went clean through the arm of a local man several of us were using as a translator. He was treated next day at a Red Cross clinic, the only medical facility that was working. The Red Cross is invariably the last to leave any conflict zone. They are the bravest.

There were United Nations personnel in Mazar and they decided the only option was to strike north towards the Oxus and hope for the best. What we definitely could not do was stay. We all assembled in a convoy of vehicles and hoped Uzbekistan could be persuaded to open the bridge before the conflict consumed us. We were all loaded up to leave, but a British TV crew was missing. We waited. It turned out they had gone off to collect a little more footage, despite endangering everybody, and had been looted at gunpoint of all their gear by some renegade group. The thieves were caught with their booty by an Uzbek militia chief who lined them up against a wall and had them shot. I think there were six of them. The TV crew begged – indeed sobbed – for the men's lives, then watched them being executed. And all for a few minutes' more of film footage. That's a hard one to live with.

We headed out in maybe a dozen vehicles, not knowing what was between us and the Oxus. It was daylight, and artillery and tanks were firing in the near distance. After an arduous journey of many hours we reached the river, but the bridge remained sealed and heavily guarded, and we could see that explosives had been laid to destroy it if anybody threatened to cross. It was also covered in large concrete blocks. UN personnel with satellite phones called their national embassies and UN colleagues in Uzbekistan to explain our plight so they could try to persuade the authorities to open the bridge temporarily to let us through.

For hours we waited, listening to the nearby sounds of war, and then truckloads of Uzbek soldiers roared into sight on the other side of the river with heavy equipment to clear the bridge so our vehicles could squeeze through. We were escorted to a dire hotel some miles away where the food looked decidedly dodgy, and I ate none of it. Those who did so fell very ill the next day. Throughout the night mosquitoes devoured us.

A UN plane arrived to take us to Islamabad and on the way the pilot received a message from Kabul Airport watchtower to land or be shot down. It turned out the UN had failed to inform the militias controlling the airport that we would be over-flying. We were kept on the tarmac for hours as groups of bearded men, upset by this perceived disrespect, argued about what to do with us. We were ordered onto the runway as this went on and there were moments when I feared for us all as tempers flared. The language barrier made it difficult to explain what had happened, but eventually they let us leave.

Never was I happier to be in Pakistan. I found a hotel and wrote a long story that ran across the top of two pages. I never returned to Afghanistan after that. I'd had enough of it. The hazard of going there had been demonstrated some years earlier when two of my dearest friends died in a helicopter crash deep in the countryside, and we could never be sure if it was mechanical failure or if it had been shot down. Sharon Herbaugh was Bureau Chief of Associated Press in Islamabad, and always the first person I visited when I went to Pakistan because her knowledge of the place was immeasurable. Natasha Singh was a young freelance journalist – still in her 20s – operating out of Delhi, and I'll never forget her excitement when she got her first important story published with her name on it. It was about drug trafficking in India, and was published in *The Miami Herald*. She wasn't working for anybody in Afghanistan. She went only for the experience.

CHAPTER ELEVEN

Bangladesh was always in a fret and fever over something, always game for a riot or mass demonstration when the mullahs wanted one, and sometimes when they didn't. You couldn't visit the country without hearing of upheaval some-where, or walking into one unexpectedly. Civil strife with several score dead was too normal to be newsworthy, and hundreds dead in yet another of its killer weather systems didn't stir much attention either. But this rather eccentric and strangely appealing country did abound in offbeat stories that commanded interest, and that's why I went there so much. These few tales spring to mind:

*Wily entrepreneurs installed satellite dishes in the slums of Dhaka, the capital, enabling hundreds of impoverished men to pay a tiny fee to gather round big TV screens to hoot, howl and holler at *Baywatch,* the like of which they had never imagined.

*Newly-arrived mobile phones revolutionised rural life by connecting every village to each other and to the world. For the first time the huge Bangladeshi diaspora had a direct link to home.

* A wonderfully restored fleet of paddle steamers, much older than the country itself, were sent off to chug around many of the country's 270 rivers, adding a spice of Mississippi romance to the hinterlands.

* A community bank gave micro-loans to poor women (typically 100 dollars) to start a business that would free them from tyrannical husbands – or the need to have a husband at all.

Those women, they were impressive, brave and inspiring. They might buy a sewing machine, a few animals to fatten or open a tiny shop, and they worked impossibly long hours in their fight for independence. Men could apply for loans too, but this was not really for them. The scheme was run by an institution called the Grameen Bank, and their loans required no collateral. It drove a social revolution, but quietly so, lest the mullahs, those splenetic old bigots, took against it. I remember a young village woman selling tiny portions of soap, spices and vegetables from a kiosk with her name daubed on the door in red paint, her pride worn with a gorgeous smile and a very attractive touch of swagger. She told me her husband had thrown her out and she had been destitute until Grameen granted a loan. She hadn't missed a single instalment, and when the loan was repaid she planned to get another and buy a cow. Her husband? 'He wants me back. I told him no.' I met another woman in another village who had used a Grameen loan to set up a public telephone kiosk using a mobile telephone. This was my take on her:

> The Bangladeshi village of Teghoria has dozens of cows, hundreds of chickens and throngs of naked children – nothing of note save for a perplexing gadget held by a woman sitting queen-like on the porch of her tin hut, which is a cut above her neighbours' mud houses. Her attitude is imperious because she is an entrepreneur. There are potted plants at the door and her chair is a rocker – grand pretentions.
>
> 'Nazma Akhter is holding a mobile phone, an addition to village life as remarkable as pukka toilets would be. Men in lungis come to her to call abroad, usually to Kuwait to talk to sons they may not have spoken to in 20 years. They watch in wonder as she dials the numbers from this little marvel. A short distance away a sign nailed to a post points down a dirt footpath towards her hut, proclaiming: 'Village pay phone.' This is the start of a telephone revolution. Rural Bangladesh is joining the world.

And those paddle-steamers: six were left out of a fleet of 56 introduced in British times and they were doomed wrecks. But they were safe, cheap and more fun than travelling by road. I went into the interior of the country on them a few times to avoid being thrown around in the back of a taxi weaving through narrow country byways clogged by buses, trucks, rickshaws and, of course, ox-carts that hogged half the space and reduced everything to a horn-blasting, furious dawdle.

The paddleboats, however, owned the waterways, obliging everything in their path to move aside as they chugged rather grandly around the country, chock-full of people who could afford the pittance-price of a ticket. One of the great advantages of these vessels was their shallow draft, enabling them to ply the most sluggish of rivers. Bangladesh insanely considered scrapping these last surviving relics, but in an inspired change of heart decided instead to refurbish them. And what a fine job they did of it.

I headed to the terminal on the Buriganga River in Dhaka to see the first example of this rebirth, and it was a glorious sight. The *Tern,* as she was named, gleamed in a new coat of bright paint, its brasses shining, the broken seats replaced, all the broken glass of the windows renewed. The engine sang happily as we waited for the off. There was a buzz of excitement as people crowded aboard and dozens of small boats milled around with sacks of cargo to be heaved aboard.

The *Tern,* built in Calcutta in 1931, was about to leave for a 350-mile trip to Khulna in the south. It was a floating imperial museum. The wheel, its blades worn thin, still bore the name on a brass plaque: Mactaggart Scott and Co, Edinburgh. The telegraph was made by Mechans Limited Scotstoun Glasgow, and still worked perfectly. The original

British built coal-fired engines were replaced by British Crossley diesel engines 40-odd years earlier, which grumbled steadily and puffed out enough smoke to justify calling the vessel a steamer. People waved and clapped on the shore as the Tern gave a blast of its ancient horn and trundled off down the river.

Bangladeshi politics were always boiling and offered ready-made stories, but this was Bangladesh so who cared? I ignored such machinations unless they erupted into something really big, and that happened over a 32-year-old writer called Taslima Nasreen, who wrote terrible books that hardly anybody read. The only one that got noticed was called *Laija,* meaning 'shame,' because it contained graphic descriptions of rape and compared men to cockroaches. Contempt for Bangladeshi men filled its pages.

But what clinched her infamy was her mockery of the mullahs. They are not people to be laughed at, and replied with a ferocious kill-Nasreen campaign, employing all their power over the masses to hunt her down. It felt like every man was now a bounty hunter, driven by clerical exhortation and ever-increasing rewards for her head. She was portrayed as Bangladesh-hating, a purveyor of filth, a woman of gross morals, a misandrist and, worst of all, anti-Islam. Her murder seemed imminent and inevitable.

It is absurdly easy to whip up a Bengali crowd. They are programmed for it. Aside from strategic considerations and an intolerable climate, the British moved the Indian capital from Calcutta (a Bengali town) to Delhi in 1931 to escape the Bengali temperament. They are fiercely political and will take to the streets in tens of thousands whenever their ire is up, and it is up a lot.

And so it happened when the mullahs whipped them into a frenzy over Nasreen. Every Friday after prayers vast numbers gathered outside the miserable apartment block in Dhaka where she lived with her mother and younger sister, chanting, 'hang her, hang her.' Posters appeared all over the country echoing this. With the entire nation in uproar she fled into hiding while rewards for her death mounted. She sent a message to Amnesty International: 'I am in grave danger. Please save me.'

I spent a week banging on doors and working the phones to try to set up a clandestine meeting with her, because it was a fair bet she hadn't been able to get out of the country. I got no closer than tracking down her brother, who told me she was switching hiding places every two or three days. For me the real story wasn't Taslima Nasreen as such: it was the extraordinary ability of the clergy to stir up an entire nation at will. The country went mad. The mullahs kept this going for weeks before deciding to wind the campaign down. The writer remained undiscovered, thanks to secret official connivance to protect her. She eventually escaped into exile, spent a decade in Europe and America, then settled in Calcutta.

This story was a rare example of Bangladesh making breaking news for something other than its weather. Some of the greatest casualty figures in the history of natural disasters have been recorded in Bangladesh and its former incarnation, East Pakistan. I went there a lot to cover weather disasters.

The place is more a river delta than a country, most of it marginally above the waterline and frequently beneath it. In 1991 it was savaged by a cyclone that killed at least 150,000 people and next day I managed to get a flight into Dhaka out of Calcutta, even though the wind was still punching wildly. I hitched a ride on a helicopter taking emergency food from the capital to the beleaguered south where the cyclone had come ashore, and the sight was appalling: mile after mile of death. Cattle, goats and people were floating in the sea and rivers, and every field was dotted with corpses and carcasses that were already bloating. Sacks of food were tossed out of the helicopter and people splashed frantically through floodwater to reach them.

Next day I went back on another aid flight, this time in a small Russian-made Antonov cargo plane. The scene was no better. The food was tossed to the ground, and as we headed back to Dhaka the weather erupted again. We were battered left and right as we approached the runway; the rain was fierce and visibility severely limited.

The pilot made two attempts to land but had to pull away. There wasn't enough fuel to reach Calcutta and only enough for one last try at landing. We circled around and dived. I was with a journalist from *The New York Times* and we were told to hold tight to a parachutists' wire called the Geronimo line, because the landing would be hard and dangerous. We were to come in extremely fast to try to beat the wind, and the undercarriage might not take the impact.

When we hit the ground with an almighty bang I saw my journalist colleague bounce up to the roof, still clinging to the Geronimo line. The plane leaped around furiously, but by some miracle we stopped without going off the runway and ploughing into the grass, which might have been fatal. The pilot leapt onto the ground and was sick.

The storm had knocked out phone communications to London, but I got through to Valerie in Delhi each night and as ever she stepped into the breach by taking my dictation and re-dictating it to copytakers at *The Times*. When I went back to Bangladesh a month later to see how the country had recovered it was as if the disaster had never happened. The poor had buried their dead, rebuilt their huts and resumed their meagre lives, as they must.

There were only two hotels worthy of the name in Dhaka at the time, standing out like braggart monuments to privilege. Next to the one where I usually stayed there was a massive slum, the stench of which hit you in the face if you opened the window, followed by a surge of flies and mosquitoes. The air pollution in Dhaka from three-wheeler scooters, open fires and scant sanitation was chronic. The traffic was a thunderous, grid-locked madness through which tens of thousands of scrawny cycle rickshaw drivers weaved in a daily death-dance – an inhumane occupation at the best of times, but in the monsoon they strained every diminished muscle to earn a pittance.

Bengalis are sociable people, friendly to a fault, but nobody would accuse them of discipline or efficiency. Nothing works in Bangladesh unless the army is involved, and even then it's hit-and-miss. Politics is a sordid affair in which plutocrats vie with mullahs, without a thought for those who suffer from their battles. Bangladesh has the worst poverty I have seen anywhere in South Asia. Begging is often an organised industry, and can get aggressive. And there is no age limit to begging.

I have more than once lashed out at gangs of children – 20 or more sometimes – in Dhaka, who would often surround any foreigners coming out of a nice hotel and menace them with probing hands and demands for *baksheesh*. It is madness to give anything: the moment you do so the throng moves in for more, and the situation can get out of control. On a few occasions I had to take to my heels until I found a scooter rickshaw to make my escape. I once took refuge in a small shop from a mob of shrieking children, and they dispersed only when the shopkeeper flew at them with a broom handle so I could summon a scooter rickshaw – 'baby taxis,' they were called – and get away. The poor kids. Parents and slum-bosses sent them out begging, and they dared not go home empty-handed.

Calcutta wore its Bengali identity every bit as defiantly as Bangladesh and had armies of beggars who were equally obscene in their brandishing of deformed limbs. Mothers were known to blind or mutilate children to make them better beggars. There were constant localised explosions of violence in Calcutta for no particular reason, just as in Bangladesh, after which life would settle back to its downtrodden, desperate and very sweaty norm. That's where Mother Teresa and her Missionaries of Charity stepped in. Calcutta's ruling elite never liked her, to put it mildly, because she associated the city with babies dumped on garbage heaps, cruel politics, brutal policing and mass poverty. Because of her that's all the world knew about the place, and nobody noticed that it was also the intellectual heart of India, the thinking man's town, the cradle of Tagore.

It wasn't that Mother Teresa didn't do good: it's just that huge numbers of local charity organisations collectively did as much, and more, without the means of boasting about it to the world. She was constantly campaigning for money that went to God knows where. I went round one of her hospices accompanied by a senior nun and was astonished at how meagre the facilities were. Where was all that money her order collected worldwide? Where were the medicines? Why were most of the staff unqualified young foreign volunteers gaining life experience for a month or two?

A journalist in America discovered that the Missionaries of Charity's bank account in New York held millions of dollars, and I asked the nun why this money wasn't being used to upgrade the hospice.

'Everything we do is according to God's instructions.'

'But where is the money going?'

'We are all children of the Lord, doing His work.'

Nothing could entice her away from this banality. I found a superb anecdote in Calcutta's main newspaper, *The Telegraph*, from a journalist who had accompanied Mother Teresa on her rounds of a hospice. This was it:

The famous nun approached a man dying of cancer.

'Hello my son, how are you feeling today?' she asked.

'Mother Teresa,' he appealed, 'why am I in so much pain?'

'Because Jesus loves you, my son.'

Long pause.

'Mother Teresa,' he responded.

'Yes my son.'

'Will you ask Jesus to stop loving me?'

She was made famous by a British broadcaster called Malcolm Muggeridge, a convert to Catholicism, who wrote a book about her with the sickly-sweet – *nauseating* might be a better description – title of *Something Beautiful For God*. When he interviewed her on television a halo appeared over her head, which he cited as proof of divinity. The cameraman insisted it was a trick of light filtering through a window.

I kicked my heels for a week in Calcutta when Mother Teresa seemed terminally ill, but she rallied. I headed back when she did die, and visited the glass-topped coffin in which she rested inside St Thomas Catholic Church. It was packed and hot from so many people, and the body was not looking good. I went back every day as thousands of people filed past to pay their respects. Calcutta's hotels overflowed with journalists and television crews – I stayed with an Indian friend because there wasn't a single hotel room available at any price – and for a few days she was the biggest story in the world.

The whole jamboree started to look grubby as her body began visibly to deteriorate, and I wrote a story saying so.

I wondered if I had gone a bit far, but it ran on the front page. I felt she was being exploited for one big final international fund-raiser, and if her feet should turn black and start to point backwards – as they did – then so what if the money was rolling in? I tried to explain India's ambivalence towards her:

> India was confused by Mother Teresa. It honoured her work while secretly hating it. An embarrassed nation felt compelled to shower awards on her. The politicians who honoured her the most were also those who despised her the most. It was their incompetence and venality she exposed, yet it is they who now shout loudest in tribute.

As soon as the funeral was over the local press felt liberated to have a go at her. The knives flashed. The *Telegraph* of Calcutta produced a withering assessment that signalled the start of dismantling the myth:

> It was the misery of Calcutta that built up and continued to sustain her reputation, that induced the rich and powerful to give her money and patronage. But Calcutta has little reason to be grateful. It was she who owed a tremendous debt to Calcutta. No other city in the world would offer up its poor and dying to be stepping stones in a relentless ascent to sainthood. Calcutta gave her a halo.

Hear hear.

CHAPTER TWELVE

I drove a steam train in India, a big black beast, decrepit, slow, noisy, and beyond filthy with the soot and grease of ages. It was one of the last steam trains to ply the Indian railways, and so ancient it dated from Raj times. It was 70 years old if it was a day. The engineers who kept this petulant thing going seemed glad see the back of it. Glad, and a touch sad.

The fireman on my particular train was not inclined to nostalgia, however. His face was pock-marked from years of being attacked by sparks. Furious red veins bulged out of his cheeks and forehead, which he wiped ceaselessly with a dirty rag in between shovelling coal into the fire. He told me in his own language – Gujarati – what he thought of the demise of steam trains, and I needed no translator. He was saying, 'good fucking riddance.'

I had applied to travel on the footplate of a steam

train to write a magazine piece about this fading piece of history, and after some weeks – things take time in India – the railway authorities directed me to a small station on a remote line in the western state of Gujarat. I headed there with my photographer, translator and friend Dayanita, who was instrumental in setting all this up: she was a brilliant fixer who could charm the most obstructive and bureaucratic jobsmith.

One hundred steam trains a month were being decommissioned and scrapped, and very soon the only ones left would be the 'toy train' narrow-gauge steam services to the old Raj hill station of Darjeeling in the Himalayan foothills, and to its southern sister, Ootacamund – Snooty Ooty as it was called, because colonial Brits frequented it.

The hill-station chuggers were kept as a concession to romantics who wanted to travel up the hillsides the way it was always done, soot and all. That's the way I went to Ooty once, sitting on a hard wooden seat, marvelling at the engineering feat of laying a track through such terrain as we wound out of the heat into the cool of this once pretty town – now a shambolic travesty. I played snooker in the former British Club on the very table where the inventor of the game had played – an army officer called Neville Chamberlain, later the British Prime Minister. My imagination conjured up images of elegant whiskered gentlemen seated in leather armchairs nursing a gin and tonic and a weeks-old copy of *The Times*.

The train I drove through Gujarat, one of the last of a steam-driven fleet of 8000, was due to be scrapped within three months when the era of steam on the world's largest passenger carrier would officially be over. She was a broken old creature for sure; the footplate was so rotten I could see the ground through it.

I arrived early in the morning and found my train grunting and panting as she was readied for a day's work, which involved lashings of grease and lots of banging and pampering and cajoling by a whole team of men. At every stop she had to be tended for some particular need. She was tragic.

We clanked to a start and rocked along, always on the lookout for cows and other animals on the track. The top speed was 25mph, which meant an average speed of 15mph with stops. Villages went slowly by and naked defecating bums shone from the fields in the morning light. There were no satellite dishes and few power lines, not a tractor nor mechanised farm machinery of any kind, just lots of slab-muscled oxen hauling carts and ploughs through the flat fields. Life moved slowly. Phones hardly existed. Electricity was scarce. I was travelling through another time, just before it changed.

The fireman barely stopped feeding the boiler. His face resembled that of a smallpox victim and he seemed immune to the pain of sparks. His eyes were devil-red. The driver, to my utter joy, asked if I would like to take control, and put a finger to his lips in a 'don't tell anyone' gesture. He placed one of my hands on the relevant handle to keep the train moving and the other on a long, curved brass lever that was the air brake, and there I was, driving a steam train in deepest India.

As we approached a bend he indicated that I should gently apply the brake. I pulled the lever down too hard, however, and with an enormous racket the train decelerated so hard it threw lots of passengers out of their seats back in the carriages. Nobody was hurt as far as I know, but plenty of people were mad as hell and came up to yell at the driver when we got to the next station.

Here are some astonishing statistics I collected at the time: Indian Railways maintained 116,000 bridges, 39,000 level crossings, 68 educational institutions, 600,000 subsidised houses for employees, 263 co-operative societies running a network of 'fair price' shops, 118 hospitals and 670 clinics. Every day more than ten million tickets were sold. This was the opening of a piece I did under a "Letter From" headline on the back page - a wonderful 700-word slot that gave foreign correspondents space to write about anything they fancied.

> Most of the 26 tribes in the mountainous north-eastern tip of India have never seen an outsider. The British sealed it off in 1873 for security reasons, coincidentally saving it from cultural destruction by Christian missionaries. The Indian government maintained the region's isolation after independence in 1947, preserving it as one of the most unexplored and unknown corners of the world. Last week the bastion fell.

I was there when it happened.

The region is called Arunachal Pradesh – in British times it was romantically known as the North-East Frontier Agency – and going there was one of the most exquisite journeys of my life. I was one of a small group of foreign journalists taken by the Indian government to have a look round after it was decided to open it up to limited tourism. Since the Indo-Chinese war 30 years earlier the ban on outsiders, including Indians, had been all but absolute. There wasn't even an airport. Little was known about the area's ancient history because scholars and archaeologists were not allowed to explore. Hardly any white man or woman had stepped foot in it for generations.

Its 52,000 square miles were home to barely a million people, predominantly of Indo-Mongoloid stock. Most were animists, with a sprinkling of Buddhists. The tribes and sub-tribes spoke at least 60 distinct dialects, limiting inter-tribal communication. Each tribe lived in its own territory, separated by mountains, forests and rivers, and generally didn't mix. Only in the foothills could they communicate in a lingua franca of Hindi and Assamese. Itanagar, the hilly capital, had a population of 25,000. There was no industry and no taxation, but I saw neither begging nor hunger. There was just one paved road that went round the state in a large circle. The rest was pristine forests and rivers.

We were taken into the interior, to a village that laid on a feast in a large communal thatched-roof building. Every item of food on the table had been grown or raised in the village. They gave us rice beer collected out of long funnels hanging from trees: water went in the top and dribbled out the bottom as warm beer. A wide river meandered by, alive with unplundered fish. The mountains loomed high, the forests were untouched, the weather was perfect, the people were welcoming, and I never wanted to leave. It was perfection.

Child labour is abhorrent, but in India it is vital. I wrestled with this contradiction in various articles on the subject and found myself at loggerheads with Christian Aid, which was campaigning against the use of child labour in the Indian carpet industry.

Under pressure from such organisations a labelling system had been established by carpet importers in Britain asserting that their carpets were free of child labour. In theory, this was a humane plan. But 4,000 miles away the law of unintended consequences was at work.

I went all over the massive northern states of Uttar Pradesh and Bihar, where many of India's carpets are woven by the poorest of the poor, to talk to loom owners, all of whom lived humbly in desperately modest villages. One room in a typical dwelling would contain a small loom. Most Indian carpets were woven on such devices. The owners were mostly subsistence farmers whose entire families weaved in winter when there was little to do on the land. They rarely had the ability to make entire carpets: they would produce a small part of it and it was assembled elsewhere into a completed product. The children in those families *had* to contribute to the family coffers by performing such labour in the off-season of farming: it was that or starvation when you lived on a dollar a day. Many of those families found themselves in greater straits because the labelling system forced them to take their children off the looms.

I talked to many small-time loom owners – peasant farmers, all of them – who had been forced to send their children to work in coal mines, fireworks factories, glass factories, truck repair workshops, or to sweatshops where they hand-rolled thin poor-man's cigarettes called *beedis* for 12 or 14 hours a day. It meant the children hardly ever saw their parents because they mostly worked in far-off places. They might be paid nothing, but at least it was a mouth less to feed. As carpet weavers on family looms they were under their parents' tutelage: as employees miles from home they had no protection, no family to turn to, no recourse if their employer beat them or forced them to work day and night. They would often end up in places with a different language or dialect, rendering them even more isolated. I met a number of them: their suffering would tear your heart out. But on the other side of the world, a lot of well-meaning people felt satisfied.

A charity I admired, and wrote about a few times because it was a stirring story, had a different attitude to child labour – namely, that it was inevitable under the circumstances. It was called 'Butterflies', and was run entirely by Indians who understood the cruel, unavoidable realities of poverty. It was based in Delhi and adopted that name because butterflies are bright and joyful and don't live long. It was a charity for child porters in Delhi railway station, a rowdy place where hordes of children worked, ate, slept and quite often died.

Butterflies set up tea-shops where porter-boys could work, rather than breaking their backs hauling suitcases. Not only that: the boys kept the profits. Each shop had a manager who might be 14 or 15 years old, and he handled everything from ordering supplies to doling out wages at the end of the day to the shop staff, who might be as young as nine or ten. These country boys had been sent to the city by their parents to find work because there wasn't enough money to feed them at home. Some who arrived were as young as seven. The only way for undernourished children so young to push a laden trolley was to do it in threesomes or foursomes, but it was still a struggle for them and it would melt a heart of stone to watch them straining.

Hordes of these boys dashed about the huge station like fireflies, swarming around anybody they saw disgorging bags from a taxi or a scooter rickshaw and fighting each other for the business. The damage this labour inflicted on them at such a young age was often visible, from bandy legs to bent backs and deformed arms. The lucky few who worked at the Butterflies teashops were desperately thankful for their lot. They knew, however, that this good fortune must end, because Butterflies was for children only, which meant that one day soon they would be cast into the real world to fend alone.

I went to prison in India, thanks to a powerhouse woman

called Kiran Bedi, who was India's most senior female civil servant and for a time head of Tihar Jail in Delhi, the biggest in India with a breath-taking 9,000 inmates, almost all men. She used to be a senior police officer and when in charge of Delhi's traffic she towed away so many illegally parked cars she became known as 'crane Bedi.' Even Indira Gandhi, the prime minister, had her bullet-proof vehicle hauled to the pound.

Ms Bedi granted my request to see her prison because, she said, she was proud of the changes she had made and was happy to show them off. She was not modest about her successes in life (which included being an Indian tennis champion), describing herself as a trailblazer for Indian women. I watched her at the start of the morning shift in her office, where she sat behind a huge desk, a tiny figure draped in an oversized greatcoat against the winter chill. She was issuing orders to an assembled cast of khaki-clad warders who clicked their heels and said 'yes madam' to each instruction.

She walked me through the prison and drew cheers from the inmates. She had recently allowed them to wear watches, a simple concession that meant a lot to men facing empty days with nothing to mark the hours. She also installed letterboxes where they could anonymously complain about abusive warders; if a particular warder was repeatedly named, she would haul him in for questioning. She introduced yoga, which was a huge success. But no matter what improvements she made this remained a terrible place, its inmates packed in cells designed for a third of those in them.

All she could do was ease the pain.

To my amazement I spotted a white prisoner. He smiled, revealing he had no teeth. His thin hair was white. He was English and had been there for ten years awaiting trial. 'I had teeth when I came here,' he said. 'And hair.' He didn't have money to oil the system so his trial, probably for drugs offences, never reached the top of the pile.

Then I saw another white face. He was English, too, called Nigel, and he had been in jail so long awaiting trial for drugs possession that he had acquired good Hindi. He became the subject of a story I wrote one Christmas. His Hindi was good enough to write a Nativity play in which he persuaded Hindu, Muslim and Sikh prisoners to participate, along with a small number of Christians. He called it *The Beginning of Life*, half in Hindi, half in English. A bishop in northern England wrote a rather passionate letter to *The Times* saying how wonderful he found it and gushed enthusiastically about Nigel's effort. 'I've been praised by a bishop?' Nigel said incredulously when I told him about this. 'That's sort of hard to believe.' I suspect he had a long crime history.

I kept in touch with him and sent a supply of something he said he desperately missed: toothpaste. And sometimes I sent a big apple pie, which Kiran Bedi sanctioned but asked me not to put a file in it. And then one day Nigel told me he had acquired money from somewhere to hire a lawyer and had been granted bail pending trial, but was not allowed to leave the country and had no passport.

He stayed with me for a while before slipping away one

night to take various buses all over northern India to make sure his trail went cold. His bail conditions meant he was supposed to report to a police station every day. I got a phone call from him a couple of weeks later: he had reached Nepal by crossing a remote border area under darkness, and was applying to the British High Commission in Kathmandu for an emergency passport. The last I heard he had made it home to England.

One of the glories of India is that nobody who follows a religious course, however bizarre, is regarded as odd. India does not in the least deserve its reputation as a spiritual country but it deserves respect for embracing those who experiment with spirituality or religion – so long as it stays apolitical. Then it can get ugly.

On trains you will meet a half-naked holy man who pays no fares because of his calling; out in the countryside and occasionally in towns you will meet a totally naked Jain walking along the road, brushing the ground in front of him with a soft cotton broom lest he step on an insect and harm it; or there will be a scantily-clad *fakir*, skinny as a stick, begging with a cup as he tap-taps along the street with his cane, heading nowhere in particular, silent as a mute. There are holy men with hair half way to their knees and fingernails half a foot long, following their particular journey; others are gloriously turbaned and painted and sit in a trance all day outside temples or at holy sites without appearing to move; and while many are fakes and chancers, most are the real thing.

That said, I did have the pleasure of exposing a cele-brated Hindu holy man who was repeatedly buried in six feet of earth for three days, only to emerge fit and healthy when he was dug out, proving to thousands of spectators that he was other-worldly. After one of these performances I jumped into his 'grave' when nobody was looking and found an opening at the bottom that led into a ventilated and illuminated subterranean cavern containing a string bed and piles of food. A pipe reached discreetly to the surface for air supply.

The ascetic who most moved me was quite a surprise. I was in southern India doing a magazine feature about a giant dam project across the Narmada River, one of India's holiest rivers, when I happened across a handsome man with a long neat beard and a cloth bag slung over his shoulder; he was meditating alone on the shore. I waited for him to stir and approached with my translator – Dayanita of course – to ask if we might talk.

'I would be most delighted to talk to you,' he said in a rather plummy accent.

'You speak English?' I inquired.

'Very well indeed.'

It turned out he was a chemical engineer from Bombay, and many years earlier he had left his family to become a nomadic holy man. We talked all afternoon: he was doing the *parikrama*, a religious ritual that involved walking 750 miles down one side of the Narmada River, then back up the other side. This would continue until he was too old or died. He slept rough or in temples dotted at various intervals alongside both sides of the river. He had given up possessions and opened his bag to show me what it contained: a comb, scissors for his beard, a piece of cloth for a handkerchief, a small mirror, and no money at all. All that he ate and wore came from alms offered in temples or by strangers. He said his parents in Bombay were well-to-do, but both they and his wife understood his need for the ascetic life. 'I provided for my wife before I left. It would have been wrong to abandon her.'

My daughter Maria was accompanying me on this trip, and we were both entranced by him. He told us he could feel the energy of the trees and the river and the animals that lived from it, and the very air dancing across the river spoke to him. 'Even the rocks we are sitting on are vibrating. Everything is energy. I feel your energy too. And your daughter's. This can only be achieved with prolonged meditation and listening.' I asked if we might stay in touch somehow, but he said no because that would mean attachment. 'I have nothing,' he said. 'Therefore I have everything.'

Nowhere in India is more remote than Jhinjhinyali, a tiny village in the desert state of Rajasthan. The people are mostly Rajputs, a warrior clan in their day. There and in villages for miles around shadowy events went on unseen. Long ago, deep in the Thar desert, the Bhatis, an elite Rajput sub-caste who used to be the rulers of Jaisalmer – now as poor as everybody else – established a tradition of murdering their mothers, wives, daughters and sisters to save them from violation by invaders. The Bhatis still killed their girls.

That was why I was there, for a magazine article about them. I saw hardly any girls in this village or any of the others I visited, so there was little doubt that female infanticide was widespread. It went on sporadically in other communities in India, too, notably in the southern state of Tamil Nadu, but here it was more prevalent.

Girls are an economic disaster for the poor because of the curse of dowry, which has become a racket that plunges poor families in debt for life. Families with daughters to marry are at the mercy of moneylenders who employ enforcers to extract payment, and rates of interest are often so high it is impossible to clear the debt in two lifetimes, so it passes through generations.

One solution for better-off women was to have an amniocentesis test followed by an abortion if the foetus was female. (I spotted a doctor's advertisement offering amniocentesis tests with the slogan: 'Better 500 rupees now than 500,000 rupees later.') Nobody in or around Jhinjhinyali had money enough for such a test, and so resorted to the tradition of murder.

I could find nobody in any village who would talk to me. The police, who never interfered much with the reclusive Bhatis, knew what was going on. 'There's no point investigating,' a policeman told me. 'Nobody ever reports a missing girl and even if they did you'd never get anybody to talk. You'd hit a brick wall.' He said there were three traditional ways of killing girls at birth: place a bag of sand over the face; stuff wet sand into the nose and mouth; or press a thumb into the windpipe.

I went to a village school where a teacher called Subash Singh told me there were 204 boy pupils and one girl. I asked him why there were not more girls. 'I don't want to talk about it,' he said. There it was: a brick wall.

There were no hotels anywhere nearby, so I slept outside on a borrowed charpoy, the ubiquitous string beds of India that are surprisingly comfortable and always flea-free (the word means 'four legs' in Hindi). There is always a *dhaba* – a roadside food stall – somewhere around to eat at, and the food is clean because it's usually vegetarian and cooked right there in front of you. I observed one strict rule in such places: wipe the plate until it's bone dry, because one drop of contaminated water will give you hell next day.

Apart from infanticide I was also working on a piece about prostitution along the main truck routes in Rajasthan, a booming industry served by entire villages devoted to it. Each village contained dozens of self-employed prostitutes, with not a grown man in any of them save for customers.

I was warmly welcomed as an outsider wherever I went. In one village they brushed down a seat for me, gave me tea, and gathered around seated in the open air to tell their stories. Lorries clanked and groaned with the coming and going of clients, and now and then a few of the women would go off for half an hour to serve them. These were fiercely independent women, never the dupes of pimps. They were born to this trade and their daughters followed them into it. Marriage was never a likely option. They felt no shame, no loss of dignity, and indeed claimed a certain status in their financial freedom.

The women belonged to a clan that used to provide dancers for the gentry but had been forced to diversify. The village I was focusing on had perhaps 20 prostitutes up to the age of about 40 – their retirement age – along with hordes of children playing innocently in the dust, not one of whom knew who their father was. The girls would join the trade after puberty and the boys left as soon as they found paying work.

The village had several mud huts set aside for entertaining men, each containing a charpoy and nothing else. There was a curtain at the entrance but no door because it was safer that way if a drunk turned violent, and truck drivers were often drunk. The price for 20 minutes with a woman wouldn't buy a cup of tea in Britain.

Dayanita and I did another story in Rajasthan that was entirely to do with rats, thousands of them, fat, twitching, arrogant, pampered, strutting, revered – and holy. They were housed in an ancient and truly beautiful temple built specially for them, with cavity walls in which they lived. They gorged sweet syrup from lots of vats set out for them.

To interview the head priest we had to remove our shoes and walk through an awful lot of rat shit in bare feet to his sanctum, where he sat cross-legged on the floor while several rats crawled all over him. The legend of the temple had something to do with a king whose son was drowned, and the king made a deal with the gods to bring him back to life. The price was that the king must become a rat.

The priest was a smiley, happy kind of man, and rats were crawling all over him all the time we spoke, including a couple that balanced on his shoulders like pet parrots. Throughout the interview one particularly large specimen kept chewing at his unshod heel, and appeared to be getting down deep. 'Doesn't that hurt?' I asked.

'A bit,' he said. 'But they love dead skin.'

There were two ways of acquiring a telephone in India: pay through the nose or wait a decade. I wanted a second phone in my office to give me a fighting chance that one of them might be working now and then. A cluster of wires hung from a telegraph pole in the street outside, a miracle of bodge-up technology that unravelled in the wind and sometimes fell off. The phone was dead as often as it was alive.

I began my odyssey at the office of the Mahanager Telephone Nigam Ltd, where I queued for two hours for an application form. The *babu* (clerk) said to go away and fill it in and return next day, which I did. Another *babu* scanned the form. 'You are needing affidavit,' he said, threw it back at me and gave me a scrap of paper explaining the procedure.

It said the affidavit must be written on non-judicial stamp paper, signed by the 'deponent' and attested by a magistrate (first class), oath commissioner or notary public. I headed to an alleyway behind Parliament Street in the centre of Delhi, where a clutch of notaries sat at tables with typewriters on them in the open air. Twenty-five rupees later I possessed the legal affirmation that I was who I said I was and lived where I said I did. Not that anybody checked.

Back to Mahanager Telephone Nigam Ltd, this time to a grey-bearded Sikh who boomed orders to his underlings like a sergeant major. He found a fault in the affidavit, which stated that I was seeking a Non-OYT General Category telephone when it should have said I was seeking a Non-OYT Special Category. He turned me away, and 200 people with application forms shuffled forward an inch.

Back to another notary, who wore a starched wing collar, from whom I acquired a corrected affidavit. The next day the Sikh snatched the document from my hand and bowed his head over it. 'It is frustrating business all this isn't it?' he said. To prove it he handed me another form and awaited its completion. 'Now you are needing magistrate to countersign. Come back with form tomorrow. You are liking India, yes?' He then took pity, cancelled the need for a magistrate's signature, and did it himself. I would get my extra phone in due course, he announced.

Many days later the local lineman came around and said he would hook up the phone straight away if I gave him money. If not, he quaintly suggested, I might wait for ever. We settled on the equivalent of £10 and the deed was done within the hour. A few days later one of the clerks I had dealt with at the telephone office sent a messenger round with a note offering his compliments in the most gushing of language, along with an empty envelope that I was obviously expected to fill.

For the rest of my time in India the lineman came by regularly on his bicycle, a skinny chap with a sweaty palm, for baksheesh. Come every Christmas I would receive a letter or two from the chaps at the telephone company inquiring about my health in the fawning manner that often characterises Indian English when in the hands of its bureaucratic torturers. It is known as Inglish. There is no language like it for lickspittling. It was not unusual to receive an official letter signed by a humble and respectful government servant asking for an early and fulsome response to his enquiries from your esteemed person in order that he might be in a position to do the needful. It was in that cringing manner that my Christmas generosity was elicited every year.

Even journalists, who should know better, were into it. I got an invitation from the Delhi-based International Journalists' Forum to a conference, stating: 'You are requested to inform about your presence in this conference by a return mail so that we are on the comfortable side to make necessary arrangements for you.' My presence, of course, would grace the occasion.

The heaving streets of Old Delhi were full of people who would normally be called weird, but in the bedlam of this ancient section of town nobody cared a jot about lots of weird people who lived and died in its fetid lanes. There were long-bearded priests, people with terrible deformities, hollow-faced men with big staring eyes who were mad with drugs, gaily-dressed eunuchs who swayed arm-in-arm

234

through the yelling and honking: the abnormal was normal.

The shortest man in the world was there and I chatted with him a few times, but he wouldn't let me write about him – although I did an obituary on him when he died. I could usually find him at his favourite teashop sitting on the counter in the corner, a cheerful character with a good line in banter as customers came and went. At just over 22 inches Gul Mohammed was too short to leap across open sewers, and would have drowned had he slipped into any of the deeper gullies. He was carried across such obstacles by whoever was at hand. People's concern for him was touching, and sometimes somebody would perch him on their shoulder to carry him to wherever he wanted to go, because dogs never ceased to menace him. When he died I wrote:

> The people of this poor and outwardly brutish section of town gave their hearts to the little man who lived mostly on hand-outs and rose briefly to fame when The Guinness Book of Records proclaimed him the world's shortest man. The walled city, with so little to be proud of, was thrilled by the celebrity of one of its own. Tea-shop owners propped him onto their counters for a free chai and the eunuchs were good friends. He had a lifelong dislike of children because they bullied him. Cats, crows and dogs were enemies, too. He would talk to the eunuchs about his dreams because they never laughed. He told them he wanted to marry a beautiful actress. To see him on the shoulders of one of these sari-clad castrated men, strong arms holding him in place, was to see

two people brought together for being different, both comfortable in this slightly insane backwater of Delhi.

I got to know several *hijras,* as eunuchs prefer to be called, thanks to Dayanita, who befriended them. They are a sometimes intimidating group who make good money as entertainers at weddings and births, and it brings ill fortune to turn them away. I did a story about a *hijra* called Mona, who was desperate for a child and paid a prostitute to get pregnant for her. Mona was a young adult when he decided to be castrated. She – as she was now called – described the horror of the back-street operation and the agony that was so bad she was tied down during it. There were no anaesthetics. She should have gone back for further procedures, but could never muster the courage.

The baby she had contracted for turned out to be a girl, and was feted by all the *hijras* in the group. She was a delightful, bubbly child, and there was fierce jealously over her. Mona ended up fighting with everybody, turned to drink for a while and was turfed out. She ended up living in the old Christian cemetery, surrounded by wild dogs. I met her there a few times and she was distressed by not being allowed to see the child. I heard years later that the girl had become a fine young woman and was married with children. She had moved away from Delhi and spurned any contact with the hijras. Mona was never invited back into the group and died many year later in the cemetery alone. The best thing that ever happened to her was meeting Dayanita, who produced photographic books about her and became her best friend. I last spoke to Mona on her mobile phone years after I left India and not long before she died, with Dayanita translating. She sounded in fine form.

Somehow I got elected president of the Foreign Correspondents' Club in Delhi, which took over my life for a while. Actually it was fun. We didn't have any fixed premises until the Government allocated us one of their old Raj-era bungalows, in which we installed a bar. This venture turned out to be quite a success for many years. That was because of the genius of its first manager, Kiran Kapur, who answered an advertisement for the job and turned up at my house for an interview that lasted precisely five seconds without a word being spoken. She stood in the doorway, smiling demurely, wearing a bright canary-yellow sari, her jet-black hair rolling shiny as silk down her back. 'You're hired,' I said, and invited her in. And thus began a wonderful friendship. I have her to thank for opening the doors to some truly wonderful people who became my friends, and for introducing me to a whole spectrum of Delhi society that I would never otherwise have known.

The club was not without its many dramas, one of which involved the resignation of the entire staff of barmen, cook and cleaners because they were terrified of a poltergeist that could be heard shouting and throwing things around the premises late at night when nobody was there. Sometimes this creature even smashed bottles on the floor. Kiran summoned a Hindu priest to do a ritual religious ceremony

– a *puja* – conducted most solemnly with incense and prayers in order to set the ghost free and entice the staff back to work. That did the job and the poltergeist never returned.

Later, we discovered the identity of the bottle-smashing entity. It was one of the barmen. He would let himself into the premises late at night with a friend or two for an almighty knees-up.

CHAPTER THIRTEEN

For 20 years a terrorist organisation called the Tamil Tigers ran an illegal, massively fortified fiefdom in north-eastern Sri Lanka on the Jaffna peninsula. It contained 800,000 people – powerless fodder for a doomed dictatorship. Everybody was a prisoner. Men, women, boys and girls were forced into war and tens of thousands died. It was an insane project initially inspired by Marxist ideology. Few journalists were ever allowed to see this dystopia, and no wonder. But I got there eventually.

The Tigers were good at killing. That was their art. They murdered an Indian prime minister, a Sri Lankan president, government ministers, politicians, peace activists, thousands of Sri Lankan Army soldiers, a lot of military top brass and thousands upon thousands of civilians – all in support of a demand for a Tamil homeland called Eelam, occupying the top right-hand corner of Sri Lanka. Tamils, mostly Hindus, had undeniably suffered at the hands of the Buddhist Sinhalese majority, and that's what drove the idea of separation. Some of the Tamils' biggest tormentors were Buddhist monks, which shocked me. I used to watch them marching through the capital, Colombo, a saffron-robed, chanting, placard-carrying baleful mob. They didn't look like they meditated or floated through life on a cloud of peace. They exuded rage and extremism, fetid and hot. Tamils were rightly terrified of them.

All my requests to visit Jaffna were ignored or rejected by the Tigers' representatives in London. Then, out of the blue, during an ultimately fruitless ceasefire agreement with the Sri Lankan government, permission came through for a small group of foreign correspondents to go there. Why the change of heart? I have no idea.

It wasn't possible to go by road, which would have entailed crossing land-mine frontlines, followed by a perilous journey through the Jaffna lagoon, a huge waterway that opens to the Indian Ocean and can get dangerously rough for a small boat. And so we were told to go by sea. We were to board a particular ship in Colombo, which turned out to be a rusty old freighter called the *Mercs Komari*. It would take us a mile off the Jaffna coast and a motorboat would collect us. We left early one morning, not a little perplexed by it all.

This ship was operated under the aegis of the International Committee of the Red Cross, and its daily mission was one of the paradoxes of the Sri Lankan war. Every evening two barges pulled up alongside it in Colombo docks and throughout the night tons of lentils, rice, grains and other basics were loaded aboard, all destined for the beleaguered Tamils in Jaffna. The government was feeding the enemy: without this lifeline there would have been mass starvation because Jaffna had no fertilisers, no electricity, no farm machinery, no seeds, and its countryside was unsafe. It was the most bizarre of charities.

We watched the last of the produce being loaded aboard and then we were off. Ninety minutes later we reached the designated spot, offshore from a little place called Point Pedro. No motorboat came for us and the sea was bucking wildly. We waited and waited, wondering if the weather had doomed our trip, but eventually a boat left the shore with two men aboard and battled slowly towards us, often disappearing among the heaving waves. When it arrived it struggled to hold its position against the freighter and we were told to hurry. A rope ladder was thrown over the side and we had to clamber down it and leap aboard. Our bags were tossed into the boat.

The first to go, an American radio journalist, dangled for a long time on the end of the ladder readying himself to jump. Timing was critical: we were told to wait for the boat to rise on the swell and leap just before it went back down. The American jumped a little too late and stumbled as he landed, and would have gone over the side but for the athleticism of one of the Tamils, who snatched him aboard. A moment later he would have been smashed between the boat and the ship's hull.

Next up: me. The rope was wet and slippery and swinging

like a trapeze. It's amazing how big an ocean-going freighter looks when you're clinging to the side of it. I let the boat rise and fall to get the measure of when I should leap, then let go. I landed OK. So did the others.

From Point Pedro we were taken in a couple of struggling old vehicles to Jaffna City, a journey of one hour on broken roads lined by smashed buildings. Nothing was entirely intact. So this was the homeland of the Tigers' dreams: it looked like a nightmare. Jaffna displayed the symbols of a country of sorts but it was all fake, a fantasy, a terrible fraud. It had its own flag, currency, legal system, police, laws and taxation, none of which had any legal authority nor worldwide recognition. Every symbol of statehood was contrived: nothing carried any authority save for the fear and terror that enforced it. Anybody who wanted to leave had to pay big money or leave close relatives behind to make sure they returned, but few ever got permission to go.

The ceasefire that had made this trip possible had been in operation for three weeks by now, but normally the territory was pummelled relentlessly by Sri Lankan security forces from the air, ground and sea. This had been going on for 12 years, with only occasional respites. The people seemed numb: there weren't many of them and they were disproportionately female or very old, because fighting-age men and youths were being fed into the war machine. I watched people shuffle through the rubble that was their lives, eyes down, rarely stopping to talk to each other, a woebegone sight.

The local police, most barely out of childhood, enforced

a 222-page penal code drawn up by the Tigers. There were small jails for those guilty of offences such as adultery and under-age sex, but there was little larceny in this crushed, lifeless place because there was nothing worth stealing.

The courts were headed by 15 part-time judges, all Tiger combatants and all in their mid-twenties. They could sentence a man to a firing squad for rape, although I was told they had done so only once. I watched the trial of a man accused of breaking some rule and the young judge looked a picture of comical pomposity in a long black jacket and formal white shirt with a wing collar and black bow tie. I hung around to talk to her. She was 25 years old and her name was Kalki Somanderam, by day a judge, by night a soldier sleeping in barracks unless she was on a combat mission. She had studied at a place with the absurdly inflated name of the Law College of Tamil Eelam, established by the Tigers in Jaffna City. 'We are guided by our leader,' she said when I asked her a question, sounding rather like a Chinese peasant bowing before a picture of Mao. To every question she gave the same answer, obviously terrified of saying something she shouldn't. The so-called defence and prosecution lawyers who presented themselves to her in court did so in a parody of courtroom formality and were so young they could have been acting in a school play.

I visited the remains of the Tamil Library in Jaffna, a hugely significant cultural and spiritual centre for all Tamils – there are 2.7 million Tamils in Sri Lanka and a staggering 70 million in India – which was burned down in 1981 in one of the worst atrocities by Sinhalese extremists. It had

97,000 books and manuscripts chronicling 2000 years of Tamil history and was one of the biggest libraries in Asia. Its destruction was a grievous blow to all Tamils worldwide, which was the point.

We were told there were 11 orphanages in Jaffna City but we weren't allowed to see them, and I can only imagine what a horror-show they would have been. Indoctrination was intense: everybody we spoke to spouted the same slogans and nobody could be enticed to go off-script. A personality cult surrounded the Tigers' founder, a reclusive man called Velupillai Prabhakaran, whose pictures and slogans were everywhere, his words quoted *ad nauseam* in the rebel-run newspaper, on rebel-run radio and on cassette tapes. These gobbets of hate revealed the murderous nature of their author, a fat-faced man with double chins and a bushy moustache. By rarely appearing in public and almost never giving interviews he maintained a powerful mystique. He was often described as a brilliant military strategist. How much brilliance did it take to blow a commuter train to pieces at rush hour?

Jaffna City, battered to oblivion, felt sinister in the unaccustomed silence of the ceasefire. There were 40-year-old Austins and Morris Oxfords that ran, choking and clanking, on paraffin, paint thinner and even, so I was told, cheap eau de cologne – and God knows where that came from.

Vegetable oil drove modified diesel generators to bring a dim light or turn a slow fan, because the Sri Lanka Government had shut off electricity supplies years earlier. Oil lamps strapped to poles provided meagre street lighting here and there. We met girls who were suicide bombers-in-waiting and boys of 14 waiting to be sent to fight and probably die, but they weren't allowed to talk to us. It didn't matter: they would have given us the usual patter.

Propaganda posters were pure *1984,* and the schools, such as there were any worthy of the name, seemed to be nothing more than indoctrination factories. The few shops contained barely more than the meagre vegetables delivered by the *Mercs Komari* every day, sanitation was bad or non-existent, and every house was semi-derelict.

This miserable place was what tens of thousands of Tamils were dying for, and for what thousands of Sinhalese were being murdered. And, as in Ulster and Kashmir, all that dying and destruction were for nothing. The Tigers were defeated in a Sri Lankan army offensive in 2009 in which an estimated 40,000 Tamil civilians died. That unimaginable slaughter rounded off the total death toll in 26 years of conflict to at least 150,000. The dead included the whiskered mystery-man Prabhakaran, who was killed while trying to escape. The net gain for all this bloodletting: absolutely nothing.

A story I did from Sri Lanka about an elephant that lost a front foot when it stepped on a landmine prompted a surprising response. It's weird, but stories like that seemed to register more with people than 50 dead in a bomb attack. I had seen the poor creature in a government-run elephant sanctuary being bullied by other elephants. When it went into the river it would be pushed over, as if to drown it – or perhaps they were just playing. Either way, it turned into a fighter and next time I visited it was being kept apart, a forlorn figure in distress.

When the article appeared a surgeon in England offered to make a prosthetic foot, and the film director Richard Attenborough offered to pay all his expenses. Alas, the Sri Lankan government wouldn't allow it. Perhaps it thought, reasonably, that humans should have priority.

The sanctuary was in a place called Pinnawala, 60 miles north of Colombo. Elephants were in desperate need of protection. Many were shot by the Tamil Tigers and others starved because of slash-and-burn farming. I watched country blacksmiths making primitive rifles that farmers bought for shooting them – brutally cruel muzzle-loader devices that fired nails, stones and pieces of metal that inflicted terrible wounds but never killed outright. There had been 12,000 elephants in Sri Lanka at the turn of the century; there were now 3,000.

From elephants to turtles. I did a story about a man who owned a small piece of beach near the south-western city of Galle that he dedicated to raising turtles, which were slaughtered in huge numbers by shipping and plunder. One six-year-old turtle was his pet, called Rosie, and she had to be kept apart because she was albino and other turtles would attack her. There was a remarkable bond between the man and Rosie, and she would rush across her tank to greet him when she heard his voice. She flapped her flippers joyously when he lifted her up out of the water – which was no easy task, because she was big.

His operation was run on a shoestring from a modest hut on the beach where he lived, but the story, some of which is here, produced a generous flow of donations that safeguarded his work.

> A palm-covered beach in south-western Sri Lanka sees a daily wonder. From here more than one million newborn turtles have scampered across the sand into the Indian Ocean over the past 18 years, saved by the dedication of one man. Chandrasiri Abbrew fights single-handed to save the loggerheads and greenbacks he loves, and little by little he is winning. Turtles once filled the local waters but were almost wiped out by the plunder of their eggs, a delicacy beloved by Sri Lankans. Now, when he dives through the coral off the small stretch of beach he owns, he sees the turtles in increasing abundance. Many know him and tolerate his touch. He looks after several turtles blinded by cats. He once found the largest turtle he had ever seen – a leatherback nearly 13 feet long, which had been injured by a ship. He nursed it and returned it to the sea.

On the occasion of Sri Lanka's 50th independence anniversary Prince Charles swept into town on behalf of the Queen, and I went there to follow him around. I couldn't imagine doing the Royal beat for a living, but there were those who loved gadding about the world writing daft stories about the royals. This visit produced its first daft story right at the outset. Charles received a 21-gun salute when he arrived at the airport, which set off a grass fire 30 yards away from him. Two fire appliances charged through the welcome ceremony and soaked everything, including the guns and gunners, who stood dripping in silent humiliation. Charles, swaddled in a suit and tie despite the tropical heat, looked bewildered and bemused by the kerfuffle and seemed to be struggling to stifle an explosion of mirth. That silly tale ended up on the front page.

I never went to Sri Lanka without meeting a delightful man called Lalith Athulathmudali, an Oxford-educated lawyer, an activist for peace, and a journalist's dream because he could deliver succinct, forensic insights into his country. He had an impressive track record: a barrister at London's Gray's Inn, lecturer at the University of Singapore, a visiting lecturer at the Hebrew University in Israel and the University of Edinburgh, a lecturer in jurisprudence at the Ceylon Law College. And yet he was the simplest of men, operating out of a modest office, always cheerful and welcoming and a little shy.

He was a politician for some years but fell out with the head of state, President Premadasa. I constantly asked Lalith why he never had a bodyguard, not even some token security presence at the door of his offices in Colombo, and he always said that if somebody wanted to kill him nobody could prevent it, so why bother? I got the impression that he fully expected to be murdered.

And so it transpired. He was shot dead in 1993. I reported the immediate claim by Premadasa's government that the assassin was a young Tamil whose body was found alongside Lalith's, dead from swallowing the cyanide capsule the Tamil Tigers carried around their necks to avoid arrest. It turned out to be a lie. An inquiry concluded that Premadasa ordered the assassination and the Tigers had nothing to do with it. The Tamil boy, it said, had been dragged to the scene and force-fed the cyanide tablet. Eight days after Lalith's murder a Tamil Tigers suicide bomber killed President Premadasa. Rough justice.

CHAPTER FOURTEEN

'He might make it.' Those are words to freeze you. 'Not' is implied. A doctor uttered them to me standing in a corridor in Moolchand Hospital in Delhi, a vast public institution of dubious reputation. Matthew was in there fighting for his life.

I was in the far north of India, in Himachal Pradesh, when I managed to call home on a bad line for a routine chat. Valerie told me that Matthew, who was 15, was extremely unwell and I immediately set about heading home. I was in the wilds of nowhere and it took two days to reach Delhi. Matthew had returned several days earlier from Karachi in Pakistan, where he had been on a sports trip. It transpired after prolonged misdiagnoses that he had contracted falciparum malaria, the deadliest form, also known as cerebral malaria because it attacks the brain. The parasites multiply at ferocious speed. Act fast, do not be old, do not be frail, or you will die. It's that brutal. More died from it than survived. Neither of the two drugs that could fight it was available in India.

Matthew had initially been admitted to a small private hospital in Delhi called the East West Clinic. Nothing they did worked because they were treating him for the wrong malaria. He needed blood, but the blood banks in India were not safe, so it had to be collected fresh. And he needed platelets, which enable blood to coagulate. There was only one place in Delhi to get platelets and that was from a government-run facility that was in chaos when I reached it. The jostling crowds were huge, the staff presence minimal, any system of giving priority to emergency cases non-existent.

I spoke to somebody who looked nominally in charge and told him my son was in urgent need of platelets. He looked at me contemptuously and told me to take my turn. What turn? How do I queue? How do I claim urgency status for my dying son? 'He needs them now,' I protested. He turned his back on me. I moved in front of him. I emphasised the urgency. 'He might die.' The words came on a sob.

'Tough,' he said, and turned away again.

I pulled him round and hit him.

All hell broke loose.

The whole pressurised room exploded. The frustrations of scores of people broke free. There was shouting and shoving and people were starting to fight each other. I cannot fully remember how order was restored, but restored it was, but what I do remember is that the man I had hit – a thump on the shoulder, that's all – was ordered by his superior to get out. It seemed he came with history.

I was asked what I needed and I showed the paperwork from the hospital. It emphasised the urgency. The platelets came.

Now for the blood. Blood from official blood banks in India could not be trusted because of poor hygiene and the tradition of buying blood illegally from professional blood donors. So that meant rallying lots of people to give an armful of fresh blood. Enter Ruth Max, wife of the redoubtable Associated Press bureau chief, Arthur Max. She was action-woman. She rang one embassy after another asking for diplomats to volunteer blood, and they turned up at the clinic in a constant procession. They came in embassy limousines and in taxis, on bicycles and by foot, ambassadors and junior clerks and everybody in between, and they never stopped coming so long as they were needed. This was humanity in action.

About a third were turned away because of dangerously high blood pressure or incompatibility. One diplomat, the second-in-charge at the Singapore Embassy, was not allowed to go home because his blood pressure was so high he could have had a stroke right there. Such is the price of the diplomatic life: too much career pressure, too much booze, too much late-night official socialising, wrested from home, unhappy spouses, dislocated children and a crap salary.

Matthew worsened. The East West Clinic was out of ideas and transferred him to Moolchand Hospital, where he was pumped with drugs, then more drugs to counter the side-effects, then more again. They were losing him. They seemed to be conducting blind experiments: pump him with this drug to see what happened and then that one, and so on. They smiled at me with that professional grin of doctors without a clue.

And then came a miracle in the form of a German doctor – Hans, he was called – who worked for the World Health Organisation. He had heard about Matthew and possessed one of the drugs that could fight falciparum malaria, which he carried for emergency personal use. He administered it and we waited. This drug was available nowhere in India because the government insisted falciparum malaria didn't exist there. The Moolchand doctors tried to stop Hans administering it because they hated to lose control of this rare case, which by now had hit the papers and was placing them in the spotlight of publicity. Pride was firmly in play. Hans administered the drug when they weren't around.

Within 24 hours the parasite was in retreat. Within 48 hours Matthew was out of danger and the hospital doctors called the newspapers to claim victory. *The Times of India* wrote a vile story saying I had refused to accept blood from Indians – quoting nobody at all to justify this. I had no energy to deal with such a scabrous insult to my Indian friends, several of whom had donated blood. I now needed to get him to London for proper care and made arrangements for him to be admitted to the Hospital for Tropical Diseases in London. Hours mattered. The British High Commissioner intervened on my behalf to delay a British Airways flight because Matthew could not wait a day for the next flight. It was Holi, a national holiday, and the hospital's accounts department was closed. The security staff wouldn't let us leave without paying, and that would have delayed us a day.

I dressed Matthew, put him into a wheelchair, and forced my way past protesting porters towards the exit door. They locked it and seized the wheelchair from me. Matthew was being flayed around. I threw a punch. More porters came, tossed me into the street and locked the doors against me. Through the glass I saw Matthew being taken away.

I ran around the building looking for side doors, but they were all locked because of the holiday. I found an open window and climbed in and found Matthew back in his room. Porters swarmed around, threatening me. I nevertheless got him back to the main door in the wheelchair. I was ready to kill. A mania had hold of me. The situation was going to get very nasty.

Then a doctor turned up, took one look at Matthew, listened to my story, and announced that he would personally pay the hospital bill if I didn't. His authority was accepted and we were allowed out. An ambulance came to take Matthew to the airport, but the driver was drunk, and I mean drunk out of his mind. Being a holiday, there wasn't another driver.

I called the British High Commissioner, who was still urging British Airways to hold the flight, and he sent his Rolls Royce limousine. Matthew was laid on the back seat and we headed to the airport. The embassy nurse offered to accompany us to London, using her own holiday time.

At the airport counter I tried buying three first-class tickets but the credit card wouldn't work because of the size of the charge, so there was more delay until I sorted that out. And finally we were off, with Matthew attached to a drip. The nurse sat next to him all the way. The plane had been delayed a long time – probably a few hours.

'I think I'm going to die,' Matthew said on the way.

'Not on my fucking watch you're not,' the nurse replied.

An ambulance was summoned to take Matthew off the plane in London, but it went to the wrong place and we waited an hour for it to find us. We went through London with the siren wailing. We stayed in the hospital for around six weeks because so many drugs had been pumped into Matthew his bone marrow seemed to be dying and he had lost most of his hair, conditions totally unrelated to malaria. Samples of his marrow were taken from his thigh with a big needle which they said would hurt. I told him a magic trick: if he imagined that my holding his hand would transfer the pain from him to me, then he wouldn't feel it so much. I swear I felt a stab of pain as the needle went into him.

Weeks rolled by. Matthew was emaciated and walked with the gait of an unsteady old man. We slept in the same room together, bonded only as parent and child can be. And one morning, very early, the main consultant looking after Matthew burst into the room in a state of great excitement. Everybody had warmed to their young patient, his irrepressible humour, his style, his courage, his character. She said his marrow was recovering and that a risky transplant from me, which was being planned, would not be necessary. He was on the road to recovery.

The Times editors were fantastic. Fruit arrived almost every day and I was told to take as much time off as I needed. When it was all over I was asked by the editor, Peter Stothard, to write about it, but I declined, saying it was too personal. I regret that. I should have written it when it was fresh, but I felt too exhausted to tackle it. When we left the hospital to return to Delhi the paper sent a limousine to take us to the airport, complete with a liveried driver. Back home, a completely bald Matthew – he had shaved off such hair that he still had – went back to school to a hero's welcome. His hair grew back. We all did.

CHAPTER FIFTEEN

The biggest industry in Phnom Penh, the once lovely French colonial city broken by years of war and slaughter, is sin. Drugs, prostitution, pornography, extortion and smuggling are the cornerstones of its tiny economy. Sex videos and narcotics are stacked in piles in local marketplaces alongside baked beans and breakfast cereals. Teenage prostitutes prowl hotels and drinking dens. Nightclubs called The Cat House and Rock Hard are raw as their names – all flashing lights, blaring music and mini-skirted girls dancing together while customers negotiate with the madam.

That was my first impression of Cambodia. I hadn't been to the Killing Fields yet. When I did so I found a giant, repellent, glass-fronted tower in which were assembled thousands of smashed and bullet-holed skulls, bits of legs, crooked arms and skeletal hands that looked like they were clawing to get out. This was meant to remind people – as if they needed it – of what happened between 1975 and 1979 when two million civilians were slaughtered by the Communist rulers, Khmer Rouge. To me it was a monument for ghouls, an insult to the people in it. I couldn't comprehend the mind-set of a society that had experienced such sickening violence and wanted to flaunt it.

I visited Tuol Sleng, a Khmer Rouge torture centre in Phnom Penh that used to be a secondary school. It is today a genocide museum, suitably sanitised for tourists. When I went there it was locked and sealed and still in its original state. A watchman took a back-hander to unlock the doors and let me have a look round. It was raw, stained and filthy, with peeling paint, broken concrete floors and leaking ceilings. It had a peculiar smell that might have been in my imagination.

I came across a metal frame the size of a double bed, attached to which were chains and a rack and pulley system for torture and mutilation. There were lots of tiny one-person prison cells, barely big enough to lie flat in, for those awaiting their fate. I entered one, closed the door and contemplated the terror of being in there for days or weeks or months, knowing that you were to die slowly and awfully and inevitably. Everybody who entered Tuol Sleng was tortured to death. Victims were told, as electrodes were attached to their genitals, not to scream when the electricity was turned on or the voltage would be increased to make it worse.

The United Nations essentially took charge of Cambodia to lead it into a fitful democracy after the Khmer Rouge regime collapsed. The UN spent an awesome amount of money and sent 22,000 personnel, called peacekeepers, overwhelming what that poor racked place was capable of absorbing. Cambodia was thrust into a world of decadence and excess, none of it benefiting the brutalised citizenry.

The UN had pulled out by the time I first visited but the soul of the country, such as was left of it after the Khmer Rouge, had gone with them, sucked out by all that UN money, all those freeloaders, all those big UN four-by-fours and nifty little private aircraft, all those peacekeepers occupying the best houses at inflated rents, all those brothels and bars that served their needs, all that cascade of indulgence feeding industrial-scale corruption and vice.

In the supermarkets, a packet of 20 marijuana cigarettes was a dollar. Guns were on open sale in the marketplaces. Prostitutes young and old walked the streets day and night. The city was littered with karaoke bars, massage joints with names like Venus and Happy World, and a sea of bleak drinking houses with low red lights and girls waiting to be taken. Many were Thai and Vietnamese.

Official privilege was on public display as air-conditioned limousines purred through rundown streets, bearing politicians behind dark glass. Among the urban peasantry many hobbled on crutches, victims of landmines – ten million were laid by the Khmer Rouge. Some of those cripples, for want of choices, formed gangs that ran protection rackets. When the UN and a host of aid agencies moved their armies of personnel out of Cambodia in 1993 – feeling they had done their job – they left behind masses of expensive gear that made its way to the black markets, including hundreds of very expensive vehicles. In the huge Russian Market I saw piles of UN radios and other technology for sale, along with pristine four-by-four cars. After the Khmer Rouge era this felt like the country was being raped again.

A year after the installation of a feeble UN-backed government, fragments of Khmer Rouge were still around, still kidnapping, still murdering. During that time I needed to get to the south of the country, and that meant driving along a country road so pot-holed it could only be taken slowly and sometimes only at a crawl. Every clump of trees or bushes might hide an ambush. The lawless countryside could still be deadly: if ordinary thieves didn't stop and rob you, there was a good chance that elements of the Khmer Rouge would. The country was still awash with guns. It was a journey of some hours but felt much longer, and the return journey lasted forever. But nothing happened. Only afterwards did I learn that the Khmer Rouge were apt to gouge out the eyes of their prisoners to stop them escaping.

I had needed to be in the south of the country to cover the kidnapping of three Westerners from an ambushed train. They had been taken to a Khmer Rouge mountain redoubt that was now surrounded by 4,000 Cambodian troops. One day there was a huge gunfight as the Khmer gunmen tried to break out but they were repelled. It was a huge international story, not because it involved a mere three foreigners but because it proclaimed that the Khmer Rouge still existed when it was supposed to be dead.

It was raining and the hostages would be wet and hungry if they weren't dead already. The Khmer 'general,' as the man heading this rump Khmer group styled himself, demanded $50,000 for each captive, to which he later added a demand for five Swiss watches. Then he wanted specific food. And beer. And more money. This went on for more than a month and the army started hitting the Khmer camp with artillery with wanton disregard for the hostages. Somewhere in his hideout in the jungles on the Thai-Cambodia border Pol Pot himself, the Khmer leader who was never brought to justice – he died old of cancer – was monitoring events.

I couldn't stay forever so I left Cambodia before the siege ended, and eventually news came through that all three hostages had been beheaded. Most of the Khmer gunmen escaped because the government had paid them the $150,000 they had demanded, which presumably provided the wherewithal to bribe army officers to let them escape.

The one sane and calm place in Cambodia at this time was the Foreign Correspondents' Club in Phnom Penh, a token name now that Cambodia had few journalists. It was known in its glory days simply as 'the F,' a grandiose colonial building that looked out over the Tonle Sap River, just up from its conjunction with the Mekong. I would sometimes have a slow meal there followed by a cycle rickshaw ride back to my modest boarding house through streets dark as pitch because the streetlights were usually off. The girls were always out though, picking their way along the ragged roads with torches in the hope of meeting a man who might not beat them up after sex against a wall.

There was a remarkable encounter on the Bridge on the River Kwai in Thailand. I arrived early for it and tension was already fizzing. Around 50 elderly and extremely agitated men were assembling at one end of the bridge while a similar-sized group of equally old men gathered fitfully at the other. Some couldn't handle it and broke down. The two groups were supposed to walk towards the middle of the bridge and meet each other, but neither seemed willing to be the first to move, and for a while it looked like stalemate. Eventually, with gentle encouragement from the organisers, the two groups began slowly and uncertainly to shuffle towards each other in complete silence save for the creaking of wooden planks that provided a walkway along the railway tracks. History was being made.

One group comprised British, Dutch and Australian prisoners tortured by the Japanese to build Death Railway during the Second World War. The other comprised some of their former guards. As a journalist covering the event I was allowed to stand in the centre of the bridge and watch each side approach in what was designed to be a ceremony of forgiveness and contrition.

A convicted war criminal called Abe Hayashi was there. He was a former Japanese platoon commander who the British sentenced to death for war crimes, but, for reasons he couldn't explain, the sentence was never carried out. He was short with thick spectacles and I couldn't stop looking at him as I tried to imagine him doing what he did. He seemed so ordinary.

His presence repelled some of the prisoners who remembered him, and they moved away if he came close. He spoke good English and said he had only been obeying orders. He told me 3,000 of the 7,000 prisoners under the command of his company died. He felt guilty for what Japan had done but not for anything he had personally done because orders were orders. He added that lots of Japanese died in Burma and they should not be forgotten either. He seemed more defiant than contrite and was causing offence. He was thoroughly objectionable. I could now imagine him with a club.

The Japanese side was accompanied by 18 Japanese primary school teachers who had brought 200 letters written by children expressing sadness for what had happened. A teacher handed these letters to one of the ex-prisoners, then hurried away without a word. Among the Westerners was an Australian woman who had come to deliver her father's posthumous forgiveness. She handed his letter to the leader of the Japanese delegation, Nagase Takashi, a former officer with the Kempeitai, Japan's military police, who bowed graciously.

He had earlier opened the proceedings at a ceremony involving Thai monks at the River Kwai Temple of Peace. 'The memory is so horrible it shames me,' he told me. One particular torture session he conducted still haunted him. Years later he sought out his victim, a Briton called Eric Lomax, to apologise. He told me Mr Lomax forgave him.

A survivor I spoke to, Dudley Cave, 74, from north

London, echoed the sentiments of almost everybody who was there. He had visited Thailand around 20 times in two decades, at first to try to come to terms with what had been done to him, and then for pleasure. 'The war was 50 years ago. I have better things to do with my life than hate. I began feeling a sense of reconciliation about ten years ago and now I'm at peace with the past.'

So there they were, tortured and torturers, shaking hands, taking photographs and trying to make sense of what each other was saying. The catharsis seemed to work for most, but definitely not for all. A Dutchman who had come to try to find some closure told me he didn't think he could go through with it. 'I feel old feelings welling up,' he said before the ceremony got under way. He broke down and left: it was too raw.

When everybody had gone I walked a long way along the railway track, which had been cut through rock and jungle in killer heat and humidity. Some of the original 250 miles of it were still in use, but trains had been suspended for the ceremony so I had the track to myself. There wasn't a sound anywhere, save for an occasional bird in the trees on either side. I couldn't even begin to imagine the scale of slaughter and torture that went on in this place: 16,000 Allied soldiers died building the railway, as did perhaps 100,000 Asian slaves who are mostly forgotten in the telling of this story.

A day before the ceremony I went to the gloriously named Hellfire Pass in a place called Namtok to meet a British veteran who was a prisoner on the railway and was determined to be on the bridge for this VJ-day event, which had been organised by the *Bangkok Post*. His name was Trevor Daikin. The former army corporal emigrated to Canada after the war and when he retired he felt compelled to live near the bridge and see out his life there. Working on the railway had been the defining event of his life. He had suffered a lifetime of emotional trauma and felt he could find peace in his old age by being there every day. He was a small man familiar in the floating bars and restaurants that clustered along the riverbank where he had lived for ten years. He was 75.

Had it worked?

'Yes. It's been a long personal journey but I'm cured.' I felt that statement was a little too emphatic. He was a nervy, timid man. His young Thai girlfriend hugged him.

In the near distance, in full sight of the little house where he lived, the recently painted bridge glinted in the evening sun. Like all veterans of the railway he hated the historical inaccuracies of the 1957 epic film *The Bridge on the River Kwai* – made entirely in Sri Lanka – that made the bridge famous, but said he was now beyond caring very much. He chugged down another beer and drew on a cigarette.

I was in Indonesia when *The Times* travel page called and asked me to do a piece on Borneo – anything at all, they said. Those kinds of blank cheques didn't come often. I hired a speedboat and went into the hinterlands where people don't normally go, dodging logs that were floating downriver from depleted forests, and stopping randomly at villages to find things to write about.

I spotted a lone thatch-roofed hut in a small clearing and asked the boatman to pull over. As I walked towards the hut a monstrous orangutan swung down from the trees and floored me with a push. It stood over me, smelly and big-toothed. This would have been a glorious way to end my life, but the creature didn't seem to have murder in mind. A man shouted and the ape ran towards him for a hug. This was the creature's master, a hermit who lived off the river and had raised the animal after finding it young and dying at the bottom of a tree. It was soppy as an old labrador and was called Marsus. I included him in the travel piece, but mostly I concentrated on the indigenous people I met, thus:

> They are no longer head hunters. The blowpipe dart has largely given way to the home-made flintlock rifle, much to the detriment of the wild pig population. And although the earlobes of elderly women reach to their shoulders, young girls do not deform themselves as their grandmothers did. The longhouse, a traditional community home for many families, is yielding to the one-family hut. Such are the changes in the lives of the indigenous Dayak in the jungles of Borneo. I found them after a long journey up the Mahakam River, in Indonesia's East Kalimantan Province. It was like the set of Tarzan. Monkeys swing through the trees and orangutans are recovering now they have official protection.

If there was one place in the world from which I would

choose to be banned it would be Singapore. I got my wish. What does one make of a country pristine as a bowling green, where toilet-flushing inspectors issued fines for not pulling the chain at public conveniences? Or which has made possession of chewing gum an offence? Or put lights and sirens on vehicles that flashed and screamed to announce infringements of the speed limit?

I was there to do a three-part series on the place and got a rare interview with the prime minister. I mostly ignored everything he said because it wasn't worth reporting, and he was very pissed off about this when the articles appeared. This was a man accustomed to dealing with the meek local press, who might ask: 'Mr Prime Minister, why is Singapore so successful?'

Singapore is of course an economic success story, but it is also true that most of the people have extraordinarily difficult lives. They mostly occupy tiny flats, have office jobs that would numb most people, and must never breathe a word of earnest criticism of the State. Crime is low, streets are clean, everything is efficient and nothing ever goes wrong: the perfect robotic society. I banged on about this sort of thing and was never granted another visa.

Looking back, my abiding image is of a country polished to unnatural brilliance, over-submissive, over-clean, over-organised, its simulated democracy checked by a straitjacket of rules and laws. No local journalist could keep his job without submitting to official controls, and no foreign correspondents could find fault if they wanted a visa to stay or return. Opposition politicians measured their words for fear of official wrath, which could involve using the tax system to bankrupt them.

The word that kept occurring to me while I was there was *bland*. Little about the country emitted any human spirit unless it was to do with trade. In that matter it pulsed with energy and innovation. The essence of the country seemed to be expressed by countless shiny shopping malls, feverishly busy docks, ships queuing miles out to sea, wide public lawns cut to perfection as if with scissors, beautiful tower blocks packed with diligent worker-armies, cap-doffing newspapers, and an intrusive, magnificently efficient bureaucracy that controlled everything it could get its hands on. Nowhere I have ever been has felt so spiritually dead.

'The Streets Where Whites Fear To Tread.' This risqué headline was in the *Sydney Morning Herald* and it offered a flutter of hope that there might be something interesting to say about Australia. I was covering a general election, and the campaign was drier than the Gibson Desert.

These apparently fearsome streets were in an area of Sydney called Redfern – an inner-city square mile of squalor – and a taxi driver said 'sorry mate' when I asked to be taken there. He dropped me nearby and pointed the way. This was an aborigines' ghetto and it was immediately familiar: the same loiterers and drunks, the same unemployed groups of men on the corners, the same dead-eyed indifference. They would not have known that they shared so much with Pine Ridge Indian Reservation 9000 miles away.

I went into a community centre whose primary purpose

was to provide a constant round of AA meetings. Alcoholism was 90 per cent. Somebody took me to Redfern radio station, a small affair run by amateurs, and I was invited into the studio to listen to a phone-in programme. Take a seat, I was told. Pop the headsets on. Have a listen.

Then I heard my name being announced. 'We've got a bloke here from the London *Times* and he's over here to cover the election. He's been good enough come and find out what we in Redfern think about it. So Christopher – what do you make of the white man's election?' I have no idea what rubbish sputtered out of me.

The streets that were fearful for whites to tread were in fact perfectly safe. Nobody had the energy or inclination for violence, from what I could tell. A couple of men sitting aimlessly on a doorstep summoned me over to chat, glad of diversion. An old woman, face and arms wrinkled like an un-ironed sheet, invited me to sit on the front step of her house. She dashed in to make tea then talked and talked and talked: and not a word did I understand. These days Redfern has become gentrified and almost all the aborigines have gone – driven out again, as usual.

I went to Alice Springs with a mind to seek out a full-blooded outback farmer for his take on the election. A hotel receptionist suggested somebody she knew and called him on his radio phone. He invited me to visit and gave directions: 'Take a right out of the hotel. Follow the road for 50 miles and take the first left. I'm ten miles down there. You can't miss my place. It's the only one there is.'

After leaving Alice, the road was dirt all the way. I had

it entirely to myself apart from a very occasional pick-up. Everything on both sides seemed dead or desperate, all the way to the horizon, which had nothing to hide behind except some twisted and shrivelled little trees. Australia's biggest battles are always with nature, and out there you see the evidence. There was nothing romantic about it: everything was stunted and in pain. The first explorers of the outback assuredly wished they had not come to that flat infinity, and it is tempting to speculate that this early disappointment helped form the slightly disgruntled nature of so many Australian men.

I found the farmer sitting outside a prefabricated little house drinking beer. I had trailed a cloud of red dust all the way, and it was still floating in the lifeless air a mile behind me. It was the only thing anywhere that seemed to be moving. He said he lived alone because his wife couldn't stand the silence and so stayed in Alice, population 25,000, which he rarely visited because he didn't like big cities. He was gruff and friendly with that inimitable Oz-man affectation. 'Stay the night if you want,' he said. 'I got two fridges. One's for beer.'

His farm was a massive expanse of scrub that could support one sheep an acre and he said he hadn't visited some parts of it in years. He claimed it was 'roughly twice the size of Singapore.' So we cracked beers and talked Oz politics. A small windmill creaked into life now and then when it found some air, sucking water from God knows where and dribbling it into a tank.

'If that dries up I'm fucked,' he mused. His views on

politics didn't stretch far beyond four oft-repeated words: 'I hate fucking politicians.' He got around to talking about aborigines and it was like listening to an Afrikaans farmer talk about blacks. The beers kept coming. 'No, mate, I don't have no blacks working for me. No better than them fucking thieving politicians. I hate fucking politicians.'

I encountered a Baptist preacher in Alice who worked with local aborigines and spoke their language. He swore a lot about politicians, too. He took me to a government housing development built for aborigines, where rows of small square houses were lined up like beach huts, every one of them empty and stripped of everything that could be removed and sold. Not one had ever been occupied.

'And that's because nobody bothered to talk to the people who were supposed to live in them,' the preacher told me. 'They didn't know that people out here live in circles. It's a social and spiritual thing. They won't live in straight lines. So the government comes along and builds everything in fucking rows a mile fucking long. Makes you want to fucking spit.'

CHAPTER SIXTEEN

I knew this phase of my life was ending. Newspapers, battered by the Internet, were cutting back ruthlessly. Foreign correspondents were being recalled or downgraded to semi-staffers called 'super-stringers.' After 20 years of solid travelling and deadline-chasing, I was weary. Valerie was increasingly sick and had perforce given up her job as head of English at the American Embassy School in Delhi. Events were closing in.

Towards the end of our time in India we rented a lovely cottage from Indian friends in the enchanting green hills in Himachal Pradesh, a five-hour drive from Delhi, where Val lived because city pollution was bad for her. I cut down my travelling as much as I reasonably could and visited frequently. She had a rare lung condition called LAM – lymphangioleiomyomatosis – which almost exclusively afflicts women and progresses slowly and unnoticed for years before becoming apparent. There is no known cause and no cure, and it eats at the lungs with the same manifestations as emphysema.

We were walking in a Delhi park one Sunday afternoon when she first said the words, 'I can't get my breath.' From that day we were constant visitors to doctors and hospitals. The disease was slow but relentless. As it progressed I began thinking of quitting my job and leaving India, but the decision was made for me.

I was just back from Pakistan when the fax message that ended my life as a foreign correspondent came through to the Delhi office. I had been to the Pakistan-Afghan frontier because an explosion of anti-Western tribal violence had endangered all foreigners in the region – hundreds of aid workers mostly, several of whom had been shot. The remainder assembled late at night for a secretive midnight convoy to safer places under armed military protection. They all got away safely. I stayed behind because the story still had life in it, and although I encountered no serious problems, the thrill of being in dodgy places was gone. It was another sign of impending closure of a way of life.

The faxed letter offered me a semi-staff position to continue as South Asia Correspondent, or I could return to the newsroom in London. I wanted neither. I didn't feel I had anything left to say about India, I couldn't stomach another trip to hotspots like Afghanistan and Kashmir, and the thought of continuing to haul myself all over South Asia had lost its appeal.

The prospect of being in the London newsroom after 20

years of freedom, and having to deal with office politics and jealousies, was abhorrent. Val's health was worsening, the children were off on their own, I was 52, and it all seemed to be coming to a natural conclusion. I had recently been nominated as Foreign Correspondent of the Year in the British Press Awards, and that felt like a high-point marker.

So I resigned. For many years afterwards I dreamed of missing a deadline, fretted that I had got a story wrong, or had turned up somewhere not knowing where I was or even why I was there. The job had entered deep into me, and extracting it was like taking a piece of me away. It took a long time to fill the space.

But neither of us ever regretted the decision. We didn't fancy returning to England, so we opted for another adventure. The world was ours: where would we go and what would we do? It was Val's idea to go to Seville and attend language school for three months, which gave rise to an excitable idea to set myself up as a freelancer covering Spain because I would be fluent in Spanish after three months, right? Dream on. But it was a thrilling dream that occupied us while we unravelled one life and moved towards another life as yet unknown – and it was delightful to be doing it in a place as exotic as Seville after so many years in the Third World.

All our possessions were shipped to Seville. It was a heart-stopping moment watching a truck take a large container of our possessions to Delhi railway station, from where it would embark on a slow meander to Bombay (later Mumbai) and thence to a cargo ship. It was due to reach

Spain within three months. We wondered if we would ever see our things again. I had heard about a diplomat who lost everything he owned when a container full of his possessions fell off a crane in Bombay into 40 feet of ocean. He had a nervous breakdown afterwards, not because he had lost all his furniture but because he had lost all his photographs. He no longer had a record of his life, and that eviscerated him.

We threw a massive farewell party in our house, at which I was given the priceless gift of a mock-up front page of *The Times*. All the 'stories' were written by journalists who had tales to tell about me – barracking stuff that I loved. The day we left our house for the last time I turned round from the back seat of the car to have a final look – except it wasn't final. We would see it again, just once.

Jamie, our dog, came with us – born in America, raised in India, and set to see out his life in Spain. We transferred flights in Frankfurt and saw him being escorted from one plane to another, and our hearts burst from wanting to go over and see him but they wouldn't let us. He came round the luggage turntable at Madrid airport in a large cage and was hysterical when he saw us. We released him and he fell over on the slippery floor. He was a cartoon dog, legs flaying as he flipped and flopped across the polished tiles to the exit, piddling all the way.

We piled into a rental car and headed off into the hammering June heat on our peregrination to Seville, taking the long road, taking time, taking stock. We called it the Freedom Drive but in honesty it was nothing of the sort. We were both afraid. The slate was blank, life had no signposts, we were jobless, youngish, and there was this feeling of time being a big empty space. There was nothing we had to do, nowhere we had to go, nobody we had to see, no phone to answer, no house to call home, nobody for Val to teach, no stories for me to write.

At our first hotel we were the only guests. Jamie was allowed into the dining room and they fed him right there next to us with a bowl of pork chops on the house. The young waitress was charming and welcoming, and we desperately needed that. We were on the edge. She seemed to see it. There are times when it's not possible to put a value on a smile or a fleeting touch on the elbow. She emboldened us. We called some Indian friends from the hotel phone because we needed that contact.

Seville greeted us as it does everybody on their first visit, by bouncing us around its narrow streets, completely lost, always charmingly misdirected because even Sevillanos are confounded by their spider-web town. Our language school had reserved a one-bedroom flat for us, which unfortunately was at the top of a four-storey building and a challenge for Val. But it was amazing: the entire roof terrace was at our disposal and the Giralda Tower, in the heart of Seville, was right there in front of us, shaking the windows with its bell-banging racket. We soon stopped hearing it. This would be home for the entire three months of our course. What happened after that was wide open.

Whoever says Spanish is easy never learned it. After three months we could barely grunt a sentence. We had spent thousands on this course and still didn't know the

word for a fork when we went to ask for one. I just don't
understand the concept of telling grown-ups they can learn
by 'immersion.' Adults have to study the damned verbs, the
future and past and present, even the hideous subjunctive.
But attending classes and plodding through the homework
nevertheless gave a focus to our existence, and when the
course was done we decided to stay on in Seville because we
had no better ideas.

We rented a huge flat in the middle of town, all five
bedrooms of it, and waited for our stuff to arrive, which
it did, on time and in perfect order. We met nothing but
kindness: Curro, the doorman, almost made us weep with
his warmth; there was Jorge, who owned a typewriter shop
across the road (the last typewriter shop in the world, I
imagine); the local barmen and women, the postman, the
young women at the supermarket checkout, the man at the
bank, the lad in the newspaper kiosk, our landlord – they
all welcomed us.

We started inviting young people to our flat for evenings
of 'intercambio' – an interchange of English and Spanish
to learn each other's languages. But we were beginning to
worry about *what next* when I got an e-mail from a publisher
inviting me to write a book about Kashmir. It was perfect
timing. Life suddenly moved into gear again. Jamie went
into kennels, we went back to India. We were happy as fleas.

And that's how we saw our old house in Delhi again,
our home for ten years. We had been away for six months
and took a taxi out to Kailash Colony to have a look at
it. It was unlocked and empty, so we just walked in. The

monsoon had come and gone, but nobody had repaired the inevitable damage. The garden I had meticulously nurtured was dead. We walked into the room that used to be our shared office and oddly neither of us could recapture any of the jubilant feelings we used to experience there. Val wandered from room to room, feeling no ghosts. The office was always the epicentre of the house, but we stood in it feeling oddly unmoved. Without furniture, without people, without context, it held nothing of us. The memories of this house had moved away: they were within us, not in this place.

It did, however, switch us into 'do you remember when' mode. There was the time when a small hole needed to be drilled into the wall for an air conditioning pipe about the diameter of a finger. There was a power cut, so instead of a drill the engineer used a sledgehammer, leaving a hole big enough for the dog to walk in and out. I had to get a builder round to brick it in.

One time when Val and I were in the office five agitated policemen burst in shouting 'blue flames!' We rushed around vainly looking for a fire. The policemen tore upstairs, still shouting 'blue flames'. Our two girls were on the roof in bikinis, sunbathing. They were terrified. It transpired that a miserable old scrote who lived across the road had decided these young ladies were making blue *films*. No fire then, just pornography.

Jamie the dog did himself proud when I was doing a live news piece for CBS Radio in America. Throughout my time in India I was their correspondent for breaking news. Even the biggest story had to be squeezed into 45 seconds because nothing must intrude on advertising time. If I'd had to report nuclear war and millions dead they would still have still cut me off after 45 seconds with 'more after these messages.' I had just started when Jamie pushed open the office door and began barking. I paused momentarily at the end of a sentence and mouthed 'shut up,' but he wouldn't. 'Happens a lot,' the CBS producer said afterwards. 'Tell the dog he's known to 20 million Americans.'

After meeting Indian friends, we flew to Kashmir and checked into Mr Butt's houseboat. We covered every inch of Kashmir, talking to lots of old men who carried history in their heads, and digging up marvellous gossip that couldn't possibly go into the book because many of the protagonists were still alive. Getting hold of the last maharajah's will and testament was an exciting coup, because it gave insight into the bitterness he felt in his final years in exile in Bombay, having been thrown out of Kashmir by India in a grubby coup. I felt a fierce and weird need to know him, and dug deeply for information. I got permission to spend several hours wandering around his long-abandoned winter palace in Jammu, enabling me to look at old photos, sit at his desk, and seek to absorb something of the man. In the end I wrote a rather fierce defence of him, despite all his well-documented flaws.

The book was published first in India and the Indian Prime Minister of the day made a speech at its Delhi launch. It also had a launch in Punjab, where I gave a press conference in Chandigarh, the state capital. That was surreal:

I had never been on the other side of a press conference before. My idea had been to write the story of Kashmir not from the viewpoint of the big powers of Pakistan and India – neither of which has a moral leg to stand on – but from the perspective of the ordinary folk of the Kashmir Valley, whose centuries of suffering are barely imaginable.

I got a deal for another book after *Faultline Kashmir* came out, looking at the history of the creation of Pakistan – which was, I always thought, an avoidable catastrophe – and trying to make sense of why it had turned out to be such a basket-case. In researching this Val and I drove through wild tribal country through the North West Frontier and right up to the Chinese border, sleeping in whatever rough-and-ready establishments we could find, and picking up a sense of why Pakistan was like it was. It was a taxing trip for her, but she wouldn't have missed it.

There was one dangerous incident. I made an international call from a phone kiosk and the man who owned it presented me with an insane bill and summoned a crowd when I refused to pay. I slapped a reasonable amount on his counter and retreated to the car, but the crowd followed and quickly became a mob. The driver froze. I screamed at him to drive off but he just sat there, terrified. The car was being rocked and banged. I slipped a couple of 100 rupees into his lap and screamed: 'Move!' That helped him find his nerve and he pulled away as his wing mirrors were ripped off and people were tugging at the locked doors. They started throwing bricks as we drove away but we escaped. Val remained cool as ice.

We got to interview – or try to – the gloriously named Wali of Swat, who was too drunk to string a sentence together. In villages way up in the mountains we came to places where people consumed nothing but vegetables, fruits and nuts and routinely lived to be 100. At one spot on this perilous road we could see three of the world's five highest peaks. And then we swung down to Karachi, a conglomeration of misery and violence, to see what people down there made of their Pakistan. Not much, as it turned out. The Muslims who moved over to Pakistan when that country was created were especially damning of it.

The book was called *The Failure of Pakistan,* and it was never released. I have one of the few copies that ever left the publishing house. The Indian Government saw an advance copy and warned the Anglo-Sikh publisher to ditch it unless I agreed to rewrite or delete chunks of it. They didn't like the fact that I painted Mahatma Gandhi as a bigot or that I had pointed out that wandering bands of Sikh terrorists, usually in small groups of five, were responsible for the slaughter of countless thousands of Muslims at the time of Partition in 1947. Their weapon of choice was the machete, the *kirpan* of Sikh tradition. I refused to change anything, so the book was binned.

Val and I had found marvellous first-hand material in lots of second-hand bookshops in the back streets of Lahore, Karachi and Kashmir, enabling us to assemble a treasure-trove of colour, background and anecdotes to put meat on the story. I loved learning from a particularly recondite little book by his personal aide, for example, that the founder of Pakistan, Mohammed Ali Jinnah, was not averse to a bacon sandwich and enjoyed a whisky, that he smoked himself to death (his preferred brand was Craven-A), that he washed his hands every five minutes when able, changed his underwear a dozen times a day, wore a white suit and tie whatever the weather or terrain, changed his shirt six times a day and never had a proper friend except for his sister, who was a dentist and lived with him.

We carried two suitcases full of old books back to Seville, where I wrote the book. Val was marvellous, as always: she went through every one of those old tomes for interesting nuggets that she would mark up for me, allowing me to pour myself into the project ten hours a day. She delved deeply into Pakistan's history and became a fantastic fact-checker. We pushed our desks together in the same room and worked as a team, totally absorbed, totally happy.

After two years Seville began to pall. It's a tourist town without a natural beating heart – all that stuff about gypsies and Jewish quarters and flamenco and horses and guitars and fiestas and bull-fighting starts to feel a bit contrived. And Spaniards are noisy. Put a million of them together in a city and they sound like a non-stop riot. Every Friday and Saturday 2000 or more young people gathered in the plaza outside our flat to drink beer and wine all night – a tradition called a *botellon*. There was never a fight, not even when a rival football team was in town, but it would go on at least until 4am throughout the summer. Before dawn half a dozen road tankers would turn up to hose down the urine, creating another hour's racket.

So we moved out and bought a beach-house in Mojacar, close to Almeria, which Val loved and I didn't. My heart lies in isolated places with wide-open spaces, where nature has room to move. That is why two years later we bought a century-old rundown *cortijo* in the countryside 50 miles away in a village called Seron. Val chose it. As soon as she saw it she wanted it. I loved it from the first day, too. Not only was it lovely; it carried phenomenal energy and had a very definite voice. I have never known a house to exude so much power.

We bought it from an eccentric old German woman, a linguist who kept switching between Russian, Spanish, Arabic, French, German and English without noticing. 'Ena,' I would say, 'you're taking to me in German.'

'Am I?' she would reply, and carry on in Russian. I asked her which was her mother tongue. 'All of them,' she said. 'Born in Germany, raised in Russia, German mother, French father, spent every summer in Spain, lived in Australia for ten years and did Arabic at university.'

The house looks out onto the Sierra de Las Filabres, which rises more than 2000 metres into an invariably blue sky. Every morning and night there is a 30-minute dance of shadows and light when sunrise and sunset turn them red and black. In Seron I felt straight away that we were at Spain's heart. I loved the rebellious spirit of country people, the feeling for family, the soul-deep attachment to culture and tradition. Andalucians are reputed to be lazy, but it's not true: it's simply that work is not their priority. Family and fiestas matter more.

For several years I wrote all the South Asian obituaries for *The Times* from our house, scores and scores of them, and while writing them I would look out of my office towards the Sierra de Las Filabres and feel very lucky to be still involved with journalism and my old newspaper. I eventually gave that up because my knowledge of South Asia and its characters was outdated, and also because Val was getting worse and I wanted my time to be with her. We travelled a lot, right to the end, because she demanded to continue with her life despite spending much of it in a wheelchair. It took a young lung specialist in a small local hospital in the nearby town of Baza to diagnose her correctly with LAM, when every other doctor Val saw in India, England and Spain said it was emphysema. She died on March 24, 2012.

And my life stopped.

Finding one's way back is an intensely personal journey through unknown country. There are no signposts, no right or wrong directions, only platitudes that mean nothing at the time but which are timelessly true, like 'you'll get through this.' Nothing about me seemed assembled in the right order any more. All that I knew, all the experiences, the growth and maturing, were replaced by childish innocence and vulnerability. It really is a process of beginning again from another perspective. Sometimes you feel you have become another person. In truth, you have.

There are times early on when normality intrudes and you convince yourself the grieving has run its course, but those moments are false friends. The wounds do of course heal and scar over, but along the way there are after-shocks that make you flinch, like damaged nerves reconnecting. Nothing compares with the emotional slaughter of the early months, when absurdly heightened sensitivities make you difficult to be around; when simple words that were never meant to be unkind fall from innocent lips as water and land on you as acid. But those pitiless days are perforce short-lived, because they would soon kill you.

In her dying days Val talked a lot about her children. Her commitment to her family was fierce. Almost her last words to me were: 'I love you Chris Thomas.' Her absolute last words were as follows, and I have them word perfect because I wrote them down in shorthand the moment she briefly opened her eyes and uttered them. They were quite astonishing. 'My mother's coming down,' she said. 'Everybody says my mother's coming down. It's very strange.' She died the next day.

My children are beyond exceptional, even adjusting for paternal pride. They cared for me during those awful days as you would a child. They made a pact to hold their grief in check at the funeral in Granada crematorium in order to carry me through it. Not one of us shed a public tear, a towering force of will for us all, but something in me, and I think in them, wanted our grief to be contained within our family. For three months a succession of true friends stayed with me in Seron, and then it was time to release them and find my way. I bless all those who held my hand on the way back.